To Joyce

07

S&S
SUPER

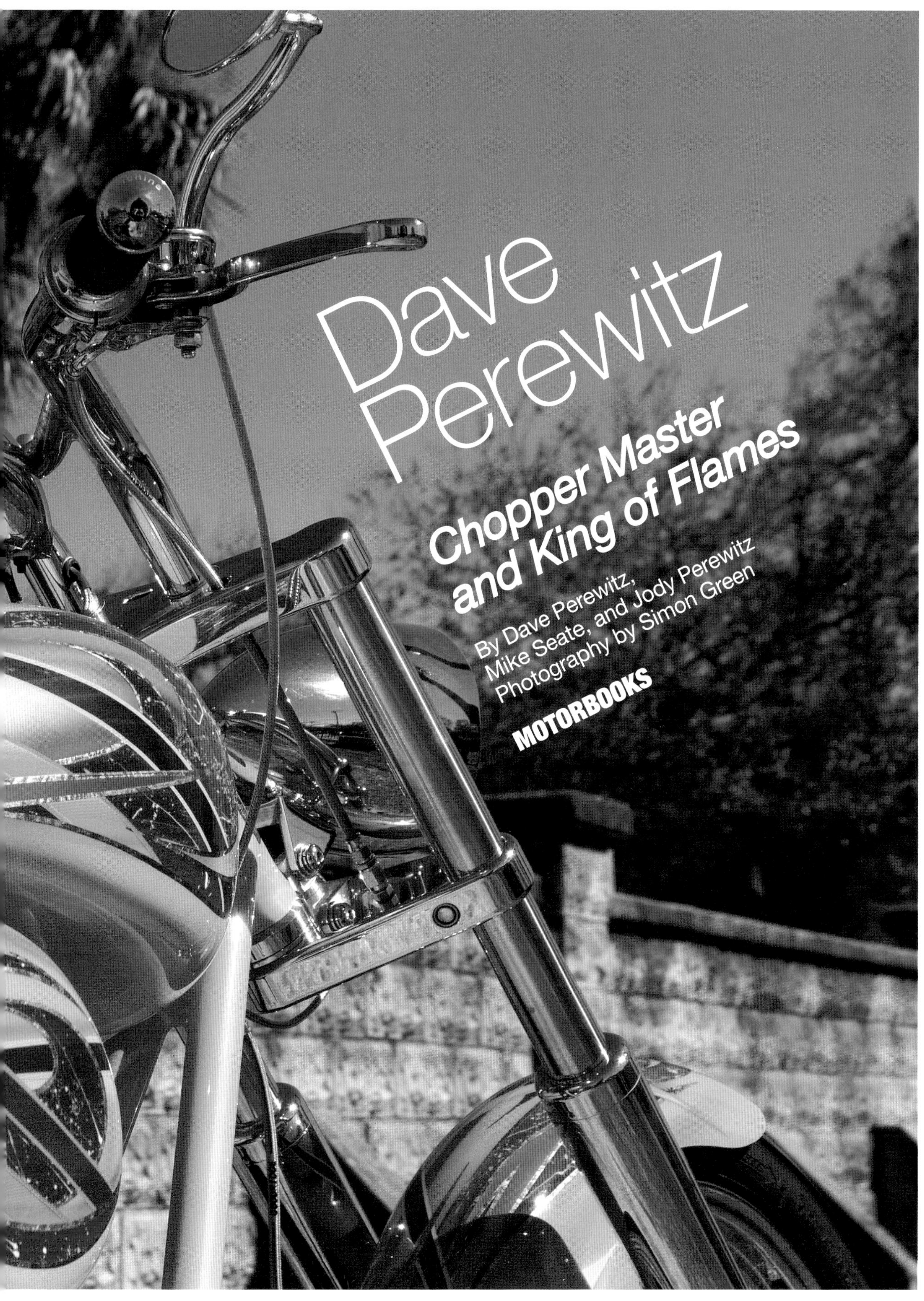

Dave Perewitz

Chopper Master and King of Flames

By Dave Perewitz,
Mike Seate, and Jody Perewitz
Photography by Simon Green

MOTORBOOKS

First published in 2006 by Motorbooks, an imprint of MBI Publishing Company, Galtier Plaza, Suite 200, 380 Jackson Street, St. Paul, MN 55101-3885 USA

MBI Publishing Company titles are also available at discounts in bulk quantity for industrial or sales-promotional use. For details write to Special Sales Manager at MBI Publishing Company, Galtier Plaza, Suite 200, 380 Jackson Street, St. Paul, MN 55101-3885 USA

ISBN-13: 978-0-7603-2384-7
ISBN-10: 0-7603-2384-4

Editor: Darwin Holmstrom
Designer: Rochelle Schultz Brancato

Printed in China

Cover portrait by Sara Liberte

Library of Congress Cataloging-in-Publication Data

Perewitz, Dave,
Dave Perewitz, chopper master and king of flames / by Dave Perewitz with Mike Seate and Jody Perewitz ; photography by Simon Green.
p. cm.
ISBN-13: 978-0-7603-2384-7 (hardbound w/ jacket)
ISBN-10: 0-7603-2384-4 (hardbound w/ jacket)
1. Perewitz, Dave, 1951- 2. Motorcyclists--United States--Biography. 3. Mechanics (Persons)--United States--Biography. 4. Home-built motorcycles--Pictorial works. 5. Motorcycles--Customizing--Pictorial works. I. Green, Simon, 1967- II. Title.
TL140.P464A3 2006
629.227'5092--dc22
2006027579
[B]

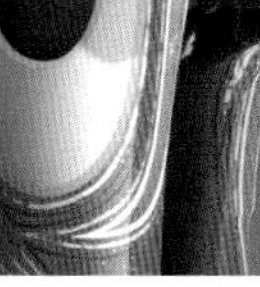

Foreword

By Bob Clark

If the custom motorcycle community as a whole went looking for a single spokesperson to represent all aspects of our sport, they couldn't do better than Dave Perewitz. Why? Not only is Dave one of the most talented custom painters and builders ever, he is also a down-to-earth, intelligent, well-spoken family man with magnetic East Coast charm. Simply put, he's good people with a colorful "been there, done that" past that has made Perewitz one of, if not the most, sought after and respected personalities in the industry.

But, it wasn't always that way. Dave's paid his dues and then some. I'd first heard of Dave back in the early 1970s. Paughco was just starting to produce the first line of true chopper components and Raja and I were building bikes at our shop, Chopper Specialties, in Anaheim, California. It wasn't until I went to work with Tom McMullen and Steve Stillwell at *Street Chopper* and *Hot Bike* magazines that I finally had the opportunity to meet Dave in person. In 1975 I'd been assigned to fly back to the Boston area and put together a feature on Dave, his paint, shop, and bikes. When I arrived it felt like home. The guy we'd been hearing so much about was painting bikes in a shed out behind his parent's house, servicing bikes in the garage, and selling parts out of a small shop on Main Street in Brockton. Within minutes of our first meeting I'd put down the camera and started color sanding a tank and fenders. Good stuff. It was during this first short visit with Dave and Sue that we realized we were family.

There wasn't a lot of money flying around in those days and just keeping the door open meant working 14–16-hour days, 7 days a week. Combine that with the borderline self-destructive lifestyle many of us enjoyed and it's a wonder Dave didn't fade into oblivion like so many other true artists of the day. Newcomers to the sport may find it hard to imagine that at one time we bikers were considered *real* bad boys, and as far as Joe Public was concerned that wasn't a good thing. To the average citizen, the term "biker" was a scary, negative term representing a darker side of society. The only time you saw bikers on TV back in the 1960s was during a televised raid on some poor schmuck's shop, when a pack of color-flying riders was caught on the open road by some news crew or chasing college coeds down the boardwalk during bike week. Those were the days that molded this sport and Dave was right in the middle of it. Truth is "bikers" for the most part were just ordinary Joes living out the fantasies *decent* citizens dreamed about but were to uptight to take part in.

Having a hard time picturing it? Try this. The year is 1980. The place, Laconia, New Hampshire. I had flown into Boston from my home in Southern California and ridden with Dave and the Cycle Fabrications crew to meet up with Donnie Smith, Arlen Ness, and Barry Cooney. Dave's wife Suzie had just given birth to Jesse and was supposed to go home that Saturday. Being the nice guy he is, Dave told her to relax in the hospital another day and he would pick her up on his way home from Laconia on Sunday. What a Prince.

Once in Laconia, Dave established a home base for us at one of the more exclusive hotels on the strip. Seaside vacationers from around the globe were caught completely off guard and daughters and family pets were immediately locked away for safe keeping. With hundreds of bikes rolling into town, Perewitz decided the long parking facility in front of the hotel would be the perfect place for an impromptu drag race, BBQ, street dance, wet T-shirt contest, and bike show. Before long bikes were lining up doing burnouts that looked like a forest fire. Run after smoking run, we began drawing spectators from all over the city. Sideline activities would have made the religious right gag and the locals dive for cover. No rules, no helmets, no trophies, no ambulance, no fuzz! It was absolute motorcycle mania of the best sort. Then just when we thought things couldn't get any crazier—make that better—Wild Man Jimmy Leahy, a very colorful and close friend of Perewitz, decided to put the icing on the friggin' cake. He walked to his room and emerged with an intimidating Naval Colt 45 revolver! Today, people would have been jumping into the bushes and Jimmy would be cuffed and stuffed. Back then the police pretty much turned a blind eye. Jimmy walked out onto the make shift track, called Dave and his brother to the line, aimed the pistol skyward and fired off a starting shot that could be heard for blocks. The crowd went wild. That pretty much set the stage for the rest of the week.

To be truthful that wasn't really anything out of the ordinary back then and it could have been just about any event any weekend anywhere in the country. That's just the way it was.

During the industry-wide slowdown of the 1980s Dave managed not only to survive but actually expanded his business. Many of Dave's one-off parts were now being licensed for worldwide distribution, his candy and flamed paint jobs received recognition throughout the motorcycle and automotive aftermarket, and custom bike journalists and entrepreneurs such as the Keith "Bandit" Ball at bikernet made sure Dave' s face and bikes remained prominent in print and later on the Internet.

When Harley made its comeback with the introduction of the Evo engine, the entire industry began a massive rebound. A whole new generation of riders, builders, and patriotic baby boomers followed Harley back and this group had serious disposable income to invest in their new hobby. They sought out legends of the custom bike world and soon Dave found himself building and painting for rock stars, movie idols, professional athletes, NASCAR teams, professional wrestlers, and major manufacturing companies. Things were looking up and the best was yet to come. Custom bikes were in and everyone who was anyone wanted a scooter.

With every other star and starlet in Hollywood showing up at local bike events on a chopper and Malcolm Forbes seemingly cruising the planet on his Harley, it wasn't long before major media organizations saw the light. Early in 2000 I was contacted by producers at the Discovery Channel regarding consumer interest in a program to be called *Biker Build-Off.* They were looking for a little history as well as current trends and names of individuals I felt would best represent the industry and be able to produce the finest in custom motorcycles within given time restraints. I put together a rough outline and list of names as requested and it didn't take long for them to recognize the Dave's potential. The rest is pretty much history. Dave was an immediate hit, the show took off, and all kind of doors opened, not the least of which was an invitation to represent the immensely popular line of PPG paint.

Regular appearances on television, at special events, and in print around the world leave little doubt that Perewitz has reached the pinnacle of his profession and he's worked and scraped for every inch along the way. Make that *they* have worked for every inch of it, because when you speak of Perewitz you're actually talking about a family unit. Suzy, Jesse, Jody, and Jaren make up the backbone of Perewitz Cycle Fab giving dad time to jet set around the globe and put a face with the name. In my estimation, if it weren't for Sweet Suzie and the kids, Dave might still be in his mom's shed. Perewitz is an all-American success story built around an entire family headed by an exceptionally talented artist and craftsman. Known to many as the King of Flames, Dave Perewitz and family represent all that is good about our chosen lifestyle (along with a little of the bad).

Bob Clark, August, 2006

Foreword

By Keith Ball

What the hell did I get myself into? Two other esteemed authors previously sequestered custom motorcycle legend Dave Perewitz in the back room of Shark's lounge in Daytona Beach and grilled him for days. Then, out of nowhere, an equally revered and hardworking editor from Motorbooks called me. "We need another foreword for Dave's book, and it better be good," Darwin Holmstrom barked, "And you have 24 hours."

"What did Bob write about?" I stumbled. "What's the title of the book?"

"What's it to you," Darwin said and I could hear him hammering his computer keyboard. He wasn't paying attention. "Oh by the way, don't call Dave. They're filming a Discovery *Build-Off* episode at his shop."

I cracked open a fresh fifth of Jack Daniels and reached for a generous shot glass in a file cabinet housing a rusting .357 Magnum revolver. I thought to myself, "Shots or take the gun and hunt down the editor?" [Editor's note: The editor has his own .357 Magnum revolver, and it ain't rusty.]

Firing up my laptop, I thought about the past. Remember typewriters, and the custom bike industry that kicked itself in the ass between '69 and '71 when Dave opened his first shop? It was a severely different time from today, an era of can-do, will-do personalities and Dave was right in the middle of the chopper battlefield. He modified his first bike in 1969 at 18 years of age. "A 1964 Sportster, serial number 64XLCH6770," Dave said. After 10 years in a parochial school, he transferred to a public institution and gave up academic classes for shop. "I discovered a welding booth in the corner used for storage," Dave said. When he indicated interest in welding, the shop professor dusted off the welding equipment and cleared the way for melting metal training.

Dave, like so many madmen of the era, learned anything and everything to do with customizing. It was all apart of the drive for freedom. The more he could do, the less he relied on others, even his supportive folks or the establishment. The era captured the essence of the American spirit. Mix that can-do desire with an artist's nature, an eye for the psychedelic, and a madman was unleashed on the growing custom world. "I never considered myself an artist," Dave said. His dad was an architect designing ships for over two decades. Although he didn't label himself an artist, he was…from the first moment he tore into a Sportster and turned it into a thing of iron beauty. "I still didn't consider myself an artist, but after a couple of decades I realized that I could visualize the final outcome. I somehow could foresee what a bike would look like from a style, shape, and color combination." That's the artist's nature, even if he doesn't realize it.

I'm not sure I can explain this, but I'll give it my best shot. Bikers were a blend of outlandish wild men, like the outlaws of late 1800s Wild West, but they weren't slugs. They created magnificent machines by day and tore into the night with wild abandon, chasing women and the next party. Dave ripped at Sportster frames with slugs machined by a friend, Wayne Burman, in his dad's machine shop. They cut the down tubes halfway to the engine. "We heated the backbone in front of the seat casting and bent it up until we reached our desired rake," Dave said. "Then we aligned the slugs with the down tubes and welded them into place."

Later they cut away the backbone of the neck and drew the entire neck back until they reached the rake they were after. No science, just welders, sweat, and an eye for perfection. Later AEE created godawful weld-on Sportster rigid sections. "We cut away the entire seat casting so the rigid tail section would align with the backbone," Dave said.

They sectioned stock parts, fabricated new components, and used whatever might be handy to take a stock Sportster and make it glisten and fly through the dark Cape Cod nights. With each frame modification Dave challenged his painting skills, like a mad chemist searching for the ultimate drug. The bikes were all stripped to the bone and batteries tossed for "the look." It wasn't about comfort and accessories, but the opposite: style and flash. "We ran only magnetos," Dave said. "There was always one bike that wouldn't start and we looked for a hill. I still check any biker's location, shop, or home for a decline for pushing a bike."

In the beginning, Dave handled every aspect of bike building from welding to sheetmetal fabrication and painting. He hung around a body shop for two years in the neighborhood. "They built hot rods and I watched them paint, until I believed I could handle it," Dave said. He painted his first bike and laid on a lace treatment. His mom supplied the lace. With each paint job he taught himself a new technique or new design. "I went to shows, spotted a wild paint job, and couldn't wait to get home and try to master it. I learned from other painters, Arlen Ness, read magazines, and checked out other builders." He never stepped into a classroom.

With a biker's nature and a family to support, Dave hit the trenches hard. He worked the shop from 9 to 6, like his hardworking dad, then hit the fabrication facility adjacent to his home in rural Massachusetts and painted three to five jobs a week, often working until 4:00 in the morning. "I had a weekly goal to deliver all the completed paint jobs by Saturday. I worked as long as it took to deliver."

In the 1980s he studied gold leafing and worked with Roy Mason. Together they sought to perfect the technique. They ran into a painter who worked with Tony Carlini in Detroit and mastered gluing the fragile leaf in place by using a clear enamel paint. "We couldn't believe how it worked," Dave said. "We also couldn't wait to try it."

Dave became the mastermind behind gun-like engraving on Harley parts. In 1977 a buddy walked into his shop with a set of engraved rocker boxes. Dave was blown away and became the builder to introduce Dick Gaudreau engraving to the motorcycle world. "He lived 15 miles away in Attleboro, near the jewelry industry hub of Providence. He was just a straight guy looking to expand his business. We ended up engraving everything. I had pallets of parts delivered from Drag Specialties, Mustang, and Custom Chrome, all the major parts distributors." Over the coming years companies complained about the prices, stole his contacts, and ultimately the engraving fad floundered. That didn't stop Dave. He kept learning, searching, and building hotter customs.

In the late 1980s Dave was faced with a changing paint world from lacquers to epoxys and urethanes. "I had to learn how to paint all over again," Dave said. "The toughest part was learning how to make corrections or repairs."

I hope (or I'll kick some ass)this book conveys that this man lived in an artist's dream world where every minute was consumed with pearlescent colors and creative endeavors. More so, even, than an animator who worked alongside the masterful Walt Disney, Dave got up every morning and faced the glory of creating something world class, coupled with feeding his family. He mixed those elements with being a biker and racing through the narrow winding streets of Cape Cod, straddling a highly modified machine of his own creation, with a bright-eyed grin on his face, and another party just around the corner. What a life.

Keith Ball, August 2006

Introduction

Dave Perewitz—Steady On

It's 1979 and a 16-year-old Pittsburgh teenager sits in his bedroom staring at a motorcycle magazine. The object of his obsession is a red Harley-Davidson Sportster in the pages of *Easyriders* magazine. The motorcycle is as raw, stripped-down, and stunning as a vintage fighter plane, its chromed and heavily engraved motor jutting out from the narrow frame that seems incapable of containing its power.

In my younger days, before I could afford much in the way of a rideable motorcycle, the thought of owning such a piece of rolling art seemed as improbable as piloting a Harrier fighter jet or scoring touchdowns in the NFL. I could have stared a hole through the thin paper of the magazine's pages—had that been possible—as I mentally stored every curve, etching, and chrome accessory on that motorcycle. The builder was one Dave Perewitz, a New England motorcycle craftsman whose work I encountered again and again in those early, impressionable years.

Through his work, Dave seemed unafraid of convention, lavishing his motorcycles with a level of beauty and sophistication rarely seen in a genre where originality is often found lacking. The engine parts were engraved like some sort of ancient jewelry, the baroque designs barely discernible from the tiny magazine images. There were deep layers of gold leaf scrollwork along the sculpted gas tanks and reworked sheet-metal fenders, creating a look that was quite a contrast to the myriad skulls, flames, and solid colors favored by most motorcycle builders.

Opposite page: **The basic formula for a Cycle Fab custom remains intact—fierce power, breathtaking finishes, and lots of style and flowing lines.**

It seemed that any type of two-wheeler was fair game for the talented Perewitz brush and hammer. We saw radical choppers he'd built from old Honda CB 750s that were as cool as anything based around Milwaukee iron, and he proved that builders didn't need to invest a home mortgage in their machines in order to make them interesting. Now-defunct magazines like *Custom Bike* and the original *Street Chopper* would frequently present Perewitz bikes in their pages. These would spark instantaneous outbreaks of intense study among me and my teenage friends, who had grown tired of seeing how the hell they did it in California and were eager to appreciate a builder from our own neck of the woods.

Time passed, and my own garage became the site of many an amateur custom motorcycle project. Like the man responsible for that first chopped machine I had spotted in *Easyriders* magazine, I stuck strictly to the Harley Sportster for a platform. Though the walloping torque of Harley-Davidson's 74- and 80-ci Big Twin motors were the powerplant of choice for most of the custom bike guys in our area, the nimble Sportster, with its almost graceful lines and uncluttered design, was the weapon of choice. And not only could you get a poorly running

Dave riding with Brian Gould, a repeat Cycle Fab customer. One of the better fringe benefits of owning your own custom motorcycle shop is test-riding the goods!

Sportster home from one of its frequent breakdowns with a roll of duct tape and a few cleverly bent coat-hangers, but the bike also was easy to customize. Even with a furniture mover's feeble salary and spray-can paint jobs, the noisy little 61-ci machines could be made to look smart and original enough to attract a few well-earned stares on the boulevard.

Years, and then decades, have passed and dozens of motorcycles of all varieties have occupied space on my garage floor. I'd always wanted to compliment Dave Perewitz on the creativity of his early motorcycle designs and, much to my surprise, I actually had the chance to do so one day. I was attending the *Dealernews* International Powersports Dealer Expo in Indianapolis, that yearly celebration of everything fast, loud, and two-wheeled. I recognized Dave from photos I'd seen in magazines over the years and struck up a conversation with him about some of the show bikes on display in the convention hall. I also excitedly spoke about that snaky little red Sportster that I'd spent most of my teen years staring at, which brought a broad, knowing smile to his face. Matching my enthusiasm, Dave eagerly discussed the details of that machine,

Dave with NASCAR legend and custom motorcycle fan Kyle Petty.

No question about who created this masterpiece—a signed gas tank is part of every Perewitz custom bike.

seemingly pleased and shocked to find a kindred spirit who could talk custom bikes all day.

Of course, as one of the world's most widely recognized and successful custom motorcycle fabricators, Dave meets people with an enthusiasm for his work on a daily basis. In fact, I almost felt sorry for him that year at the Indianapolis show as I watched dozens of well-meaning fans crossing his path, shaking his hand, complimenting his work, and generally offering props.

But as I watched each and every visitor pass his way, I noticed something. Nowhere to be seen in Dave's persona was the cocky, swaggering stance of the latest generation of made-for-TV chopper stars. If there was a conversation Dave didn't enjoy having, you wouldn't have noticed it from the friendly smile and the unmistakable New England accent. The man behind the bikes many of us loved was as genuine and interesting as his designs. And that's something you can't buy from a catalog.

After getting to know Dave a little better through interviews for articles I'd written for the custom Harley-Davidson magazine *IronWorks*, I realized that Dave's trajectory in the motorcycle world was a unique and inspiring tale all its own. Though riders had been altering their machines since the earliest days of the twentieth century, Dave's entry into the chopper game happened to fall at precisely the right time: he was a young adult in the psychedelic 1960s and had firsthand experience watching customized motorcycles as they emerged from the cultural shadows and became pop culture mainstays.

Because he chose to pursue a career in custom motorcycle parts fabrication at precisely the same time that a nation—and later, a world—developed a thirst

The crowd gathered at a typical Cycle Fab Bike Night at the new Bridgewater shop.

for altering its motorcycles, Dave Perewitz was onboard for a ride that the motorcycle industry is still enjoying. And thanks to his memory and the work of dozens of dedicated photographers, the whole crazy story with its unrelenting long hours, its technological innovations, and its unrivaled creativity are here for all to see. And who knows, maybe before we're through, Dave will show me how to build a proper version of that little red Sportster after all.

Chapter One

Humble Beginnings

Above: **The name that launched a thousand gaping jaws.**

Left: **From a humble 12x12 shed, Dave Perewitz's Cycle Fabrications has grown into the Northeast's premiere custom motorcycle powerhouse.**

I guess you could say that motorcycles were definitely not in my family's blood. A lot of custom bike builders will tell you they had fathers or older brothers or uncles or somebody who rode bikes way back when, but for my family, nothing could have been farther from the truth. My family, like most in our area, was the completely conservative stereotype family from that era. It was like the cast of *Leave It to Beaver*; my Dad was an architect who worked in an office every day from nine to five, the whole family took a two-week vacation every year, and like clockwork we ate dinner at 5 p.m. every night.

I didn't really know anything about custom bikes back then, and neither did my friends, who started out hot-rodding cars. From about the age of 12, I loved cars and would walk Main Street in Brockton and watch all the cool hot rods drive up and down all evening, cruising for girls and making their tremendous noise. I was hooked, but at that age, all I could do for a few years was build model cars and dream at home. Later, I got hooked up with a bunch of older guys who had hot rods. I'd met them in town hanging out and they helped me to get started with my first car, a 1956 Corvette I co-owned with my mom, from which I first learned how to hop up and maintain my only ride.

But just like today, kids will be into something one minute and then something entirely different the next, so by the time I was 18, all the guys with hot rods had suddenly switched to motorcycles. It wasn't because they'd seen some

Opposite page: **Custom pro-street rides are now available made to order at Cycle Fab.**

movie or read about it in a magazine, it was just the next cool scene and the new thing everybody just had to do. Even though we lived near Laconia, where they'd had the rally for years, we hadn't really been aware of motorcycles like kids are today with TV and the Internet and all the magazines. We actually saw bikes on the roads only very rarely, but when we did, we remembered every detail because the sight of somebody on a motorcycle was incredibly cool and the unpredictable weather in New England made riding tough.

You have to remember that bikes were a lot different than they are now. The first bike I bought, at the age of 18, was a 1964 Harley-Davidson Sportster. It was 1969 and it was 800 bucks and that was a lot of money in those days. The Sportster was the high-performance bike back then. It was really fast and didn't look like anything else on the road, so naturally it was the bike that everybody younger than 30 wanted to have.

It's funny how you see so many Harley-Davidson Big Twins in the custom magazines nowadays, but back then, all you really saw were the Sportsters or old panheads. Us young guys always thought Sportys were so much cooler because they were skinny and had this lightweight feel to them, while the Big Twins were considered touring bikes for those old guys. I got my first Sportster and right away decided to totally rebuild it, even though I didn't know a thing about customizing motorcycles. I had spent a lot of time hanging around a local auto

From a humble 12x12-foot shed, Dave Perewitz's Cycle Fabrications has grown into the Northeast's premiere custom motorcycle powerhouse.

"I'll always stop and sign autographs for people. I'm just glad people care enough to appreciate what I do."

Previous page: **While many custom builders turn their backs on stock Harley-Davidsons, Dave enjoys the challenge of tricking out the occasional bagger.**

Top: **Early Triumph Bonneville–powered custom built by Dave when his shop was still located in his family's backyard work shed.**

Bottom: **Early Perewitz "digger"-style custom based on Dave's favorite powerplant, the Harley-Davidson Sportster. His longtime buddy Arlen Ness helped popularize the low, narrow machines.**

"You mean this thing has a second gear?" Dave has a laugh after riding a wild-looking Strochek Sportster-powered kit bike. During the 1970s, anything and everything was chopped.

body, Tarky's Autobody shop, where I'd managed to learn a few things, especially the basics of painting and body work, so some buddies and I tore that Sportster down and started working on everything.

It's also funny that today guys who want to get into building custom bikes can just buy a book or a video and study how to do it. The best teacher is experience, not a book or video. I've met guys who said they got into building choppers because they'd seen it on the Discovery Channel's *Biker Build-Off*. The way we learned back then was trial and error for many years. When I started painting bikes I used the same techniques as the guys in the bodyshop. Over the years I developed my own techniques for bikes.

When I started on my 1964 Sportster, it helped a little that I'd actually seen one of the first custom paint jobs a few weeks before, when a guy named Paul Gamache pulled up to the local watering hole driving a 1964 Ford station wagon he'd recently painted. I know that doesn't sound like a very cool car, but he'd custom painted the hood with some brilliant design and we were all blown away that somebody could take an ordinary grocery-getter and turn it into something completely unique.

Although guys like Von Dutch were already operating on the West Coast and we'd all seen cars by Ed "Big Daddy" Roth, custom painting was just coming into play back in 1969. There was very little of it on the East Coast at the time,

By the late 1970s, Dave had moved to his Brockton, Massachusetts, location. A burgeoning chopper parts aftermarket filled the walls with bolt-on accessories.

but a couple guys had tried it with good results, so I figured I could do it too. Keep in mind that at the time, even though Roth's *Choppers* magazine had hit the West Coast and *Street Choppers* started about a year later, in 1970, Roth's magazine was hard to find. They didn't provide much of a guide for those who wanted to customize a bike. It's safe to say we were all pretty much on our own.

When I painted my first bike, my dad had a little shed for his lawnmower in the backyard that was maybe 4x10 feet, tops. I needed room to paint the bike, so I took everything out of the shed, bought a DeVilbiss spray gun (one of the best ever made), just started playing around, and painted the bike. I actually ended up being fairly pleased with how it turned out. I did the whole thing in black pearl lacquer (it seems like all paints were lacquer back then) and then took a piece of lace—which I had picked up from the fabric store my mom shopped at—masked it to the bodywork, sprayed some silver through it, and that was it. Everyone liked the paint job and I ended up riding that bike all that season.

At the time I was working as a line mechanic at a Chevy garage. I started painting bikes for my friends whenever I could, but no one ever made any money

Dave and Susan enjoy happy times at the Brockton shop as business continues to grow.

painting bikes back then. An average three-piece paint job for bodywork and paint, one color, was about $35. There were a few chopper shops, but they were all run by older guys. I didn't know these guys, so information was hard to come by.

When the next year came, I had some new ideas I wanted to try. I tore apart the Sportster again. I did my second custom paint job on the bike. This time, I decided on a candy red with airbrushed cobwebs. The whole thing ended up with a multitude of colors, because there were really no rules about what made a cool chopper; you just made it up as you went along. About halfway through this project, I decided to try to make it into more of a chopper-style bike. I realized I'd picked up enough knowledge working as a car mechanic that I could weld, work with sheet metal, and do anything else necessary to create my own chopper.

If you wanted to extend the front end on a bike back then, you had two options. One was to extend the front end by purchasing slugs, which were just short, machined pieces of steel that you put in under your stock fork tubes. These were really dangerous, because the forks could hit a bump and literally

The hell with California! Cold Northeastern winters gave Dave plenty of time to design and build motorcycles for the coming spring.

Bikes like this digger Harley-Davidson Sportster landed the Perewitz name in national motorcycle magazines frequently during the 1970s.

Multilayered ribbon paint on this peanut gas tank was time consuming to apply, yet fetched few dollars during the 1970s.

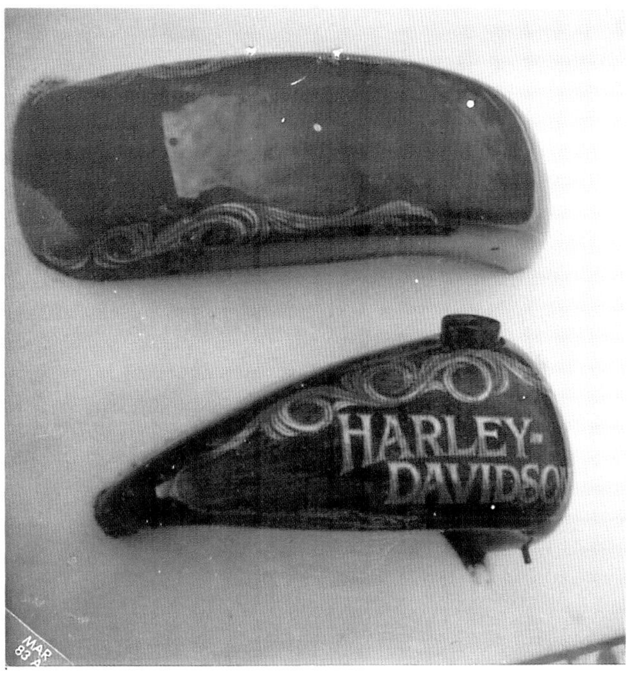

Because many Cycle Fab customers could not afford full-blown custom bikes, Dave became an expert at tricking out factory parts like these Fat Bob tanks.

Gold leaf detailing is a Perewitz staple, a process he learned to admire from studying antique fire engines.

just pull apart. The other way, if you were lucky enough to have a local chopper shop nearby, was to buy a springer fork or a set of extended tubes. I decided a pair of 6-inch over fork tubes was the way I was going to go. I made a custom seat and sissybar. Paint, extended front end, custom sissybar and seat, and straight pipes were the modifications I made to my bike that year.

I couldn't wait to take my new bike to Laconia 1970. My bike was a big hit. I was on my way home from Laconia and I saw what appeared to be a really cool chopper in my mirror. I slowed down so that the guy could catch up to me and as he rolled by me I saw the coolest chopper that I had ever seen. I remember it like it was yesterday. It was a long, stretched-out rigid frame about 20 inches over springer with a custom baby-blue paint job. I looked at the guy as he was next to me and gave him a nod as he passed by. I knew then that I was going to make my bike as cool as the one that just passed me.

I couldn't wait for the weather to get cold so that I could tear my bike down. As soon as the leaves fell, my bike was completely apart. I cut the neck off

Excellent view of a trio of Cycle Fab original customs during the 1970s—drag bars, king and queen seats, and chrome ruled the day.

the frame and extended it 12 inches with 40 degrees of rake. I got rid of the swingarm and shocks and welded a hardtail on. I mounted the Sportster tank high on the top rail, Frisco style. I put a 19-inch over Mothers Springer with buckhorn bars. Now I was on my way to that cool chopper I wanted. I painted it Aztec gold with multicolored ribbons. When I showed up in Laconia that next year I definitely had one of the coolest choppers up there!

Looking at the custom show bikes today, it's hard to believe how hard we rode those choppers back then. It was nothing to spend all winter building a bike, and then ride it all year, and in all kinds of weather. For one, we didn't really have a lot of money back then, so if you had put all your bucks into a bike, you rode it because you couldn't afford anything else. My chopper was a big hit and a local guy ended up buying it for $2,400, which was big money back then. I kept that bike for three years and was sorry to see it go, but it was time to move on.

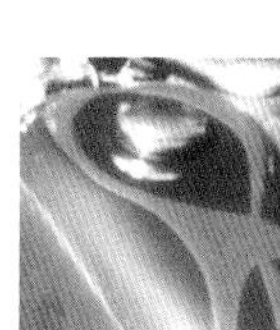

Dave endures the unenviable job of judging the machines on display at a Daytona Beach bike show. Check out the vintage hot pants!

I was lucky to have a friend named Slick from Boston who knew a lot of guys with bikes, and when somebody needed money, Slick would set me up to buy them out. One day in 1971, Slick called and said he had a guy in the Bronx with a few bikes in parts for sale, so we drove down there one Saturday in my old van. When we finally got to this guy's house, it was right in the middle of the ghetto. The man we came to see wasn't home, so we sat for about four hours waiting for him. It was pretty shaky, with all kinds of people walking by, staring at us. When the guy finally showed up, he was really nice and it turned out he had a ton of stuff to get rid of. I bought a garageful of parts and two whole bikes for $1,200. We went back home and I built my next custom entirely out of the stuff I got on that trip.

To be honest, when I look back on those early days, I never thought I'd end up doing this for a living. It was more of a hobby. But after awhile, guys would see something I'd done—a sissy bar or a flat-bottomed gas tank or a fender on one of my bikes—and the next thing you know, I'm in my dad's

Dave Perewitz, circa 1984. "I never expected to get famous or make any money from building motorcycles back in the early days. I just did it because it was fun and I loved doing it."

Detailed view of the intricate finishes Dave put into his Sportster customs. Check out the blue anodized wheel rims and intricate engraving work on the fender rails.

basement welding or brazing a piece of steel and selling the parts. Just about everybody had stock bikes back then, and the Harley-Davidson dealerships didn't stock custom parts. A lot of dealerships wouldn't let you in the door if you had a custom bike; they only allowed stock bikes. It wasn't something I thought would make me rich; it was just fun and a challenge to see what I could make.

Imported bikes were getting really popular, and the guys who owned them wanted cooler-looking bikes but were at a big disadvantage, because the import dealerships didn't deal with the whole chopper thing just yet. I did quite a few customized Japanese bikes in the early 1970s, when Honda's CB 750 and Kawasaki's Z1 came out. Those bikes were very popular because they were super fast and very reliable, but there weren't many parts around for them. We did a few of them after Arlen Ness started making custom frames for Japanese bikes. He made weld-on, raked front sections that could make an otherwise stock motorcycle look like a radical chopper, as well as full-on rigid and Softail-style

continued on page 38

Customizing choppers didn't always pay the bills at Cycle Fab. Everyday service of road bikes was, and still is, a shop staple.

Origins of the Species

Though it seems difficult to imagine in today's top-dollar, high-profile custom motorcycle market, many builders' careers started off by focusing on a single machine at a time. Money, not a lack of creativity, was the principal reason the early custom motorcycle shows were generally filled with builders displaying one machine each. And that bike, often a motorcycle ridden regularly and aggressively on the street, was the sole focus of that builder's acumen for many years at a time; the same bike was customized over and over, year after year.

Dave Perewitz was no different, purchasing his first Harley-Davidson, a 1964 XLCH Sportster, from wages he'd saved while working in a Chevrolet repair shop in his native Brockton, Massachusetts, in the 1960s. Deploying an impressive 55-ci displacement and an easy-to-access 50 ft-lb of torque, Harley's smallest V-Twin made an excellent platform for custom builders looking for speed and style.

In its earliest incarnations, Dave's first custom project bike bore the look of a pure East Coast street chop, circa the Psychedelic Era: the front forks was extended 6 inches via a set of lengthened, lathe-machined fork tubes, a rare find in those days. The front fender was removed while the stock, 19-inch wheel with its massive drum brake remained intact. A set of wide, buckhorn handlebars replaced the flat-track-style bars that Harley-Davidson had originally supplied, and the rider sat proudly on a riveted cobra seat, complete with a funky hex-stitching pattern. With several years of bodyshop experience under his belt, Dave stenciled this bike with his first-ever flame paint job, a fairly modest orange pattern laid down over a metallic blue background.

As was the style in those days, a thorough session in the bodyworking booth followed any chassis mods. The welds and imperfections were covered with dense layers of Bondo putty. The stock telescopic forks were now gone and an early Springer front end from Paughco sat in its place, deploying a corner-challenging, 19-inch extension. Likewise, the handlebars continued to contort into ever more complicated combinations of bends, and the throttle side was bereft of a front brake lever.

Dave freely admits that bikes like these handled with all the grace and agility of a Safeco shopping cart, but with little known about chopper frame dynamics (besides what individual mechanics deduced from trial and error and the occasional involuntary "landscaping" session), nobody seemed to mind the odd fork flop or handlebar wiggle. The rigid rear section of the chassis was also a weld-on bit, topped by a king and queen seat, which now somehow looks as dated as a pair of platform shoes decorated with peace signs! Despite having to pull double duty as Dave's everyday ride and test bed for new designs, the bike turned out to be a show-winner at venues all over the country for several years.

frames for 750 Hondas. It wasn't until a few years later that you could buy custom Mustang tanks or chromed hex oil tanks and organ pipes for the imported bikes. Until then, you had to make all that stuff yourself, and it was very labor intensive.

Even when I was doing more custom bike work, it was a long, long time before I said to myself, "This is what I'm going to be doing." I was still living at home and working on paint jobs and bikes for 14 hours a day. The demand was getting stronger for my paint jobs.

In 1971 I built my first shop with the help of my father and my friend Connie Lyons. The new shop was a little bigger than a one-car garage. Half was a spray booth and the other half was for fabricating, assembly, and whatever else we had to do. Now I was in the big time. My prices went up on paint jobs; for a frame, tank, and fender, multi colored was around $150. My old man turned out to be pretty supportive. My folks were behind me all the way, though my mom kind of freaked when she saw my first tattoo—moms will do that!

I also worked some very long hours back then, and that's sort of carried over to my career today. The norm was always about 80 hours a week, and now the average day starts at something like 8 in the morning and I'm usually just finishing up by 10 at night. I haven't worked a 40-hour week since I got out of high school. People always ask me how I can work so hard all the time, but the

Dave looks resigned to a long day of hard work on this fire-damaged dresser.

CYCLE FABRICATIONS
erewitz
Custom
Motorcycle Accessories

A Perewitz rear fender, fresh from the fabricator's hands, on its way to a customer.

only answer I have is that I truly love motorcycles. I love the business and everything about it. I love being able to do all the stuff that everybody dreams of doing, whether it's trying out my ideas on a real bike or test-riding something that has taken months to build and perfect. Even after 35 years, when I get up in morning, I can't get to work fast enough.

I look at some of the bikes I see on display at the shows and I realize how many guys are doing this who really aren't dedicated and don't put in the hours necessary to do a really good job at it. There's a real problem with custom bikes today: people want to build bikes because they think it will get them rich or make them famous and they'll be on TV, but those are the wrong reasons for trying to do this, and it shows in their work. Back then you had to do it all yourself and as a result, most of the guys building custom motorcycles and parts had a background in automotive mechanics or engineering. They knew how to do things right because they learned the hard way.

Here, Dave's son Jesse, age 8, gets an early start learning the custom bike game. By the age of 14, Jesse was working regularly in the shop.

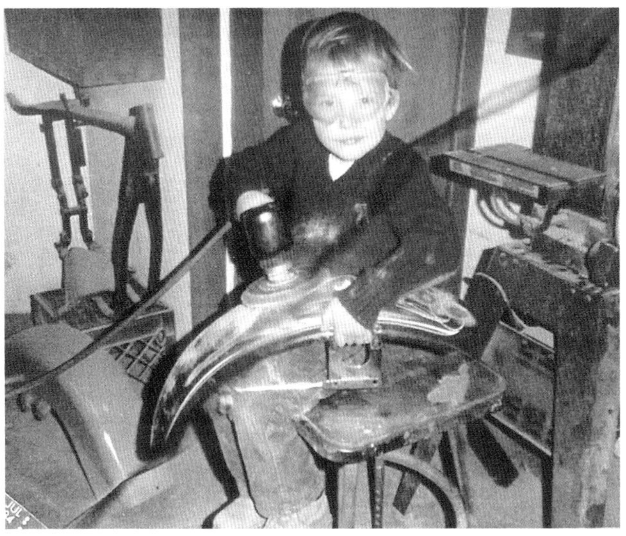

I attended my very first custom bike show in January 1974. This was a big show, the first of its kind up in Boston at the Commonwealth Pier. It had been advertised in the Sunday paper for a month, and the organizers promised that whoever won the "Best Bike in Show" trophy would also win a new Harley-Davidson Sportster. Everyone I knew who had a torch and a spray gun was busy getting their bikes ready for the show, and we worked for months detailing our entries and getting everything straightened out over the winter. My entry was a 1964 XLCH I'd been riding hard that season.

I entered my bike into the show and it was a huge success, though not without a little drama. When the doors opened on Friday night, the promoter thanked everybody for bringing their bikes out and proclaimed that the owner of the best bike would get a gold watch for first prize. A little confused, we politely reminded him that he'd promised a new Sportster, but he refused to honor his word even after one of the guys showed him the newspaper ad with the new Harley in it.

We were all local guys in the show and we stuck together. We had all worked really hard and each of us wanted a fresh bike to start cranking on, so on Saturday, we banded together to get our Sporty. At 7 p.m. the place was absolutely mobbed, with a line of people waiting to get in that stretched two blocks down the street. Just as the crowds rushed in, all the bike builders covered their motorcycles with blankets so nobody could see them. The promoter caved in then, and said he'd come up with the free bike for the show winner. I won the show and the 1974 Sportster. I ended up selling it for $2,800 and heading straight to Daytona a couple of months later with the same bike I'd used to win the show.

I was always eager to get to Daytona after a long winter, and I still am. It was great to see what everybody else was building. When you look back, people

now would be surprised at how few guys had custom bikes in the mid-1970s; there were only a couple of stretch choppers at the shows or one or two parked outside the motels. You definitely didn't see the wild, European choppers; the guys from Japan; and the rest of the world coming to Daytona on radical bikes back then.

In 1974, I hung out, rode my show bike around Daytona, and ended up meeting a guy named Joe Alphabet from Alphabet's Customs; he'd originally came from near me in Connecticut and was pretty successful at making exhaust headers. I won the Rat's Hole show in 1974 and Joe was so impressed he talked me into going to a show in Detroit soon after. Joe was a great guy who loved to have fun and ride. He was living in L.A. at the time, where he'd done pretty well with custom van stuff, which was also very popular in the 1970s. Joe was the first big-name guy I'd ever met, and we got to be good friends.

One day, my friends and I were in the shop reading *Custom Bike* magazine. We all agreed that our bikes were good enough to be in a magazine. I took the

Opposite page: **Dave and fellow biker Dave Nye soak up some sun in Laconia, 1977.**

Right: **Dave taking care of business at his shop in the early 1980s.**

phone number out of the front of the magazine and called the editor, Larry Kumferman. I told him that I was a kid from the East Coast and had a cool bike that I thought should be in his magazine. He asked me why I thought my bike deserved to be in a magazine. By the end of our conversation, he had agreed to come in two weeks to photograph several bikes I had built. The first time one of my bikes appeared in a magazine was in 1974; from then on it was tough to *not* see my bikes or name in a magazine.

In April of 1975 I went to a show in Detroit; this is where I first came into contact with the guys who really loved building custom motorcycles and made a living at it. The show was easily the country's biggest. All of these wild builders and characters I'd heard about in the magazines or through the small-custom-builder's grapevine were there. The bikes were crazy, with lots of regional tastes and touches I'd never seen before.

At that show I met Arlen Ness, Ron Finch, Tony Carlini, the Yosemite Sam Brothers, and two of my best friends, Donnie Smith and Ed Kerr. I won first in my class and best paint in the show. Arlen Ness and I became friends and I invited him to Laconia. He shipped his bike out to the East Coast we had a great time. After Laconia, Arlen asked me to go to Detroit with him and hang out with the bike builders out there and ride our bikes. Arlen told me something that was very important: when you meet people on their own level it makes a huge difference. Being in Detroit with Arlen put me at the same level with the

other builders. It is something I have always remembered and applied not just in the motorcycle world but in everyday life.

By 1975, custom motorcycles were rolling, with all kinds of people riding bikes. There was lots of coverage in the magazines by then, and all of the sudden, *Street Chopper* was easy to find. People were customizing everything they could get their hands on, even little commuter bikes like Honda CB 350s and 450s and British bikes like Triumphs and BSAs.

In Detroit and the Midwest, they had these big Bondo machines with sculpted gas tanks, molding, and wild paint schemes. There was always inspiration to try new stuff. I had kind of adopted the Bay Area style with the really skinny look, which later became known as the "digger"-style choppers.

Being friends with Arlen Ness was a huge inspiration. His creativity was endless. He has always been very likable and as nice a guy as they come. Arlen was very helpful when I needed to talk shop or ask for advice about opening my first store.

All those legendary guys were there, including Arlen Ness. We met at that show for the first time and right away became good friends. To this day I don't think there's anybody out there with the creativity that Arlen has.

Back at home after Detroit and Laconia, the shop was going full bore, and I continued to progress in my work. I had good support from my mom and dad,

Opposite page: **The Perewitz family gathers for a group portrait. Clockwise from left: Dave, Jody, Jesse, Jaren, and Susan.**

Dave's very first Harley, a 1964 XLCH Sportster, shown here packed and ready for his very first trip to Laconia in 1969, would launch his career as a custom bike builder.

which was a huge help. I also received lots of help from my friends in the media. Custom motorcycles were still too underground to be of much interest to people who didn't ride bikes. I had my brother Don working with me, doing molding and prep work, and still we could hardly keep up with the demand. I met my wife, Susan, in 1970, and she wasn't into bikes at all, but she used to come to my dad's house and hang out while we worked. She eventually bought me my favorite Christmas present in 1971: an airbrush that I'm still using to this day.

My first bike appeared in *Easyriders* magazine in 1976. It was a yellow Sportster with a raked Ness front section and, let me tell you, it was a massive thrill to see one of my bikes in *Easyrider* magazine. I was painting bikes and building choppers pretty much full time. I was pretty focused. I received a lot more recognition from that *Easyriders* feature, but the custom bike craze still wasn't all that huge by then. I never wondered if this was the right direction to go; I just did it.

One guy who was a huge influence of the popularity of my bike was Bob Clark, the editor of *Street Chopper* magazine for 22 years. I met Bob in the mid-'70s and we became the best of friends. He used to travel with us to most of

Opposite page: **This is the same machine, two years and many long nights later. Builders in those days often redesigned a single bike for several years.**

the major events. He is a great guy and was very generous with his magazine by covering what we were doing at Cycle Fab. With Bob's help I was on the cover many times. His magazine was one of the best and few means of reaching people in those days. Back then, there wasn't TV or the Internet like shops have today. We would print Cycle Fab T-shirts to give away, hoping that people would see them.

After hooking up with Arlen Ness and spending so much time with him, my bikes took on a serious Bay Area style. They comprised a very long, low, stretched-out, and skinny frame with a short springer front end and a spool wheel up front, and a big, fat, 16-inch tire in the rear. The gas tanks were either stretched Sportster tanks or a diamond tank that looked almost delicate. I recall people latched on to the nickname "needle-nose" because those bikes were so skinny. That look appealed to me because, even though they were all over the West Coast, it was still really unusual in the Northeast. I'd generated a lot of press and a reputation for building good, reliable customs, and I opened my first real retail store (with Arlen's help, of course) in 1975.

Arlen really had to push me into opening the store. He was one of the first guys to make his own mass-produced, custom, aftermarket frames, gas tanks, and front sections. It may be hard to imagine anybody doing this for somebody today, but when I first opened the store, Arlen sent me a bunch of his custom

Opposite page: **The very first flame paint scheme that Dave laid down using a spray gun that his wife, Susan, bought as a present. Not too bad for a beginner!**

parts to stock and said simply, "If you sell it, pay me." We built a lot of Ness-style lowriders and diggers. I often wonder now where all those bikes went, because you know they're out there—you just don't see them anymore.

The storefront took a few years to catch on, but I was one of the only shops in my area and was definitely the only one stocking those one-of-a-kind parts. It would be a number of years before people at shops all around the country were able to order from Drag Specialties or Jammer's Handbook, though there was a custom parts supplier named Gary Bang from L.A., who was a great guy and sold good, well-made stuff. He was one of my main suppliers. I used to look forward to opening boxes that I knew were full of parts from Gary Bang. Years later, Gary and I met and we have become good friends since.

We were having fun at the store, customizing everything from Harleys to Hondas—and even a BMW—but we sure weren't making any money at it. The surge in chopper popularity was still a few years off and the work was labor intensive, so margins were slim. And by the early 1980s, I had a family to raise, on top of everything else.

Opposite page: **Extensive molding work performed on the radically raked chassis on the 1964 Sportster. Most of the accessories were handmade in those days.**

Next page: **Dave Perewitz with friend and fellow Hamster Dave Silvia.**

Chapter Two

Above: **Intense scrollwork like this takes hours to apply and decades to perfect.**

Opposite page: **The Magna Cycle was sold as a kit during the 1970s. Dave bought this bike in 1974 from Arlen Ness, rode it two years (often riding two-up with his wife) and sold it. He bought it back in 1999 and restored it.**

Fabulous in the 1980s—Hard Work and Hard Times

LINCOLN ELECTRIC
USA
ROGO
FASTENER CO., INC.
1.800.423.ROGO
LINCOLN ELECTRIC

I had ended the 1970s on a pretty big high. I had bought my first house, and by 1980, Susan and I had our first child. That year, I'd finally taken the time to build my first complete shop on our property and, at last, had enough room to really stretch out and start doing all kinds of work that I'd always dreamed about. I'd need the extra room because, by the 1980s, the way people viewed custom bikes had changed. That year I also moved my little retail in Brockton to a 1,000-sqaure-foot location on North Main Street.

In the 1980s, builders were starting to slip into the more high-tech market trends and bikes had to have things like electric starters and disc brakes—things everybody takes for granted today. Bikes were no longer quite as long and skinny as they had been, either, with more people getting Big Twins instead of Sportsters. This was quite a change for me, because as I'd mentioned earlier, ever since the late 1960s we'd been operating in a sort of regional status and everyone around New England had Sportsters.

As I got to travel more, meet more people across the country, and see more custom bikes built around Big Twins, I had no choice but to start following the new progression of customs. This all happened at the same time Arlen Ness started making a name for himself as one of the real leaders of the Big Twin movement. He was always at the forefront of things, and this time he was busy making really cool frames for Harley-Davidson's Big Twins that used swingarms,

Opposite page: **Customer care doesn't end at the check signing; Cycle Fab bikes get serviced by the crew who designed and built them.**

which was a real departure from the hard-riding rigid frames that we had been using. I was very eager to try his new chassis out.

Mechanically, the new decade was a tough transition because the new technology made it harder to make a bike look really skinny like we used to make them. And folks weren't as interested in skinny by 1981 or so. People coming into the shop had seen the Fat Bob bikes and were hooked on the new style, so we started broadening our horizons. Where we had used simple magnetos for ignitions, we now had electric starts that required bigger, more powerful batteries to crank 'em over. I'd always thought the cool thing about the smaller, skinnier choppers was how much lighter and faster they were. Plus, if you ever needed to push one after it broke down, you would have appreciated the lighter weight!

I think one of the first real signs that things had changed in the custom bike world was Harley-Davidson's release of the FX Wide Glide with black

King of his own castle at Cycle Fab during the 1980s.

paint and flames in the 1980 model year. It was pretty incredible the way it produced basically a stock bike with a flipped rear fender, chromed bolts, and a lot of other stuff no one had ever seen on a factory bike. That bike even had a wide glide with a twin-disc front end that I remember everybody wanted for a project bike.

On the other hand, there were guys who didn't like it because it was obvious that the factory had copied what bike builders were already doing . . . but then again, when you think about it, manufacturers have *always* copied the custom guys. It's become common; they do it even more so nowadays and everybody expects it. But way back when, the factory guys were watching guys like me and Arlen Ness and Donnie Smith to see what we were doing. It's too bad the factory never really bothered to actually work with the custom bike builders the way automotive manufacturers did with the car customizers. In fact, as far as I knew, the people from Harley-Davidson never worked with us on *anything*, with the exception of a few small projects with Arlen Ness and Al Reichenbach.

If you looked along a timeline, my bikes' popularity and recognition didn't go up a lot in the 1980s. Looking back, that's probably because I was raising a

The best of both worlds: Dave finishes his lowered Chevy Suburban and a cool FXRS custom in the same shade of red.

ALLIED
MAR

Opposite page top: **This ultimate digger Sportster made *Easyriders* magazine in 1979 for its wild engraving, cut-down bodywork, and the world's first show-chromed turbocharger.**

Opposite page bottom: **Never a fan of long front ends, this Perewitz Sportster utilizes stock-length forks and a steering damper.**

Above: **With a young Arlen Ness in the background, Dave checks out the seating position on a typical 1970s chop—dig those crazy rigid struts!**

The Perewitz fall Foliage Run has brought Hamsters members together from around the globe while raising tens of thousands of dollars for charity.

Dave and pal Donnie Smith share a laugh while working together.

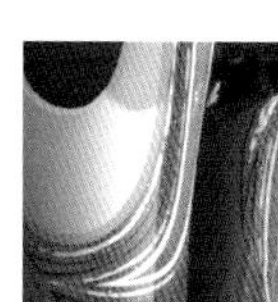

family, which took up a lot of my time. I had three kids, which put me in a different place and different frame of mind. I was still building and custom-painting motorcycles, but I wasn't as aggressive as I might have been. During the '80s my main focus was on custom paint. We were still showing up in the magazines every so often, and I was pretty well known when I'd ride one of the bikes I'd built to Laconia or another big show.

Motorcycling as a whole was becoming slightly more acceptable, but there just wasn't the kind of widespread interest in choppers that you see today. Customs were still such a minority in the motorcycle world that most of the guys building choppers all knew each other by first name. In some of the bigger towns, even the guys who just had a passing interest in custom bikes knew each

continued on page 66

Riding Hamster

A lot of people don't know this, but I'm one of the original Hamsters. There have been a lot of stories about how it all got started, but the truth is that Arlen Ness, Donnie Smith, Barry Cooney, Ed Kerr, and I were vacationing down in Daytona during Bike Week in 1978. My old friend Jim Leahy was there, and the whole Hamsters name grew from a joke that he kind of started.

We were riding every day and partying hard at night, and Jim had a slang term he used—sort of as a term of endearment for his drinking buddies—and he'd look at you and say, "You fucking hamster," or, "What a bunch of hamsters you guys all are." It was just one of those funny things people say when you're out having a good time, one of those funny things that kind of sticks in your mind and makes you laugh. One night, Jim and Susan were left behind, so they were pissed off at the guys. When we got back to the hotel, Jim and Susan had woken up and drawn a picture of a hamster and stuck it on everybody's door. From then on, the name just stuck.

We had our first official Hamsters run later that year in Sturgis, and Donnie made these silly yellow shirts, and it really took off from there. We've managed to be in Sturgis every year since, as Hamsters. People always thought up goofy garbage like "to join the Hamsters you have to wear the same socks for two days in a row," and stuff like that, but basically it was just a bunch of guys who liked custom bikes and wanted an excuse to get together and ride. There's no special initiation rite to join or anything.

It's come a long way since then. There have been documentaries about us on TV, and now the Hamsters have about 250 members worldwide, including England, Japan, and Italy. The foreign chapters got started when Arlen Ness met some builders and custom bike guys from Italy who came over to ride with us and, from then on, the Hamsters were officially world travelers. Hamsters are a great bunch of guys; everyone helps each other out. Most of the top bike builders in the world are Hamsters.

I'm always amazed at how popular the American custom bike scene is with the Europeans, especially since we never really gave much thought to their custom bike scene. I think they like the fact our society is so much more open to customized motorcycles in general. It's a lot freer over here, because European authorities restrict a lot of the modifications bike builders can make. They even have restrictions on what they can do to modify their front ends in Germany, and builders have to subject their bikes to the TUV tests for safety. So in recent years, we've become good friends with riders from Germany, Australia, France, and all sorts of places.

I'm glad those guys come over to ride with us on our turf, because I don't travel overseas much anymore. I guess I just don't like being somewhere where you don't understand the way the money works. In fact, you don't really understand anybody at all because we all speak different languages and come from different social backgrounds. I've done my share of traveling in Europe, I guess, and I get offers to go over all the time, but I prefer it back here at home.

A few of my bikes ended up overseas and have made some pretty exotic stops along the way. Just recently, I built a bike for a guy in Australia, who came all the way over and just shipped it back to the island, which is pretty wild. I've also built a couple of bikes for a guy in Aruba, which is about the last place you'd expect there to be custom motorcycle guys. He got the bike I built him back to the Islands, and apparently people there are so enthused about it he wants to put on his own custom bike show. I guess the custom motorcycle thing has caught on with people everywhere.

So, to join the Hamsters, it really doesn't matter where you're from—Aruba, Australia, America—you just need to be a builder or serious custom bike enthusiast. You have to like to ride your custom bike. And you have to like having fun, like all the rest of us "fucking hamsters."

The least-scary motorcycle club insignia in all the world!

This sculpture is one of many pieces of original art that Dave has collected from other Hamsters members.

Left: **Minnesota's Donnie Smith, a founding Hamsters member and longtime friend and contemporary of Dave's.**

Opposite page: **Inside the inner sanctum at Cycle Fabrications, where the Hamsters are never far from reach.**

other, there were so few of them. That could be a plus, though, because if you needed something welded, you knew who the welding guy was. If you wanted something painted or some molding done, that guy was friends with so-and-so, who rode with somebody else, and inevitably you knew who he was and where to find him.

Though I slowed down a while to raise my family, from about the late 1980s on, I became more and more aggressive, and the popular response to my bikes increased as I learned how to work the industry. My main source of income at the time was paint jobs because we didn't make shit selling off the show bikes we built. All through the 1980s I was doing anywhere from three to five paint jobs a week, working 12- to 14-hour days with a staff of just me, my brother, and a guy who did artwork for us. We were really busy all the time. I was lucky that

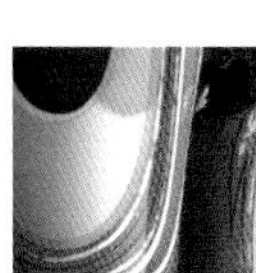

the shop was built on my home property, for otherwise I would have seldom been at the house. But we were close by, so if I needed to be with my family or there was an emergency, I was right there in the yard. Susan would come out to the shop at night just to spend some time with me.

One of the techniques that I really focused on during this period—and one that became something I was known for as a builder—was incorporating gold leaf into my paint. This is something that originated with fire-truck lettering. I'd always noticed the way scrolls really set off the detail work on those old red fire engines, and figured I could apply that technique to my bikes and really make them stand out.

When we first started doing the scrolls, some of the original designs we used were from—believe it or not—dollar bills. If you hold a dollar bill up to the light and study it, there's a lot of elaborate scrollwork on it. We just copied some of the designs, enlarged them so we could see them better, and started using

Megaphone pipes; wide, 5-gallon Fat Bobs; and serious passing-lane speed were must-haves for the 1980s.

them for the patterns that ended up on our bikes. It was always time-consuming work that added days, sometimes even weeks, to the work on a bike. But nobody else was doing anything like it at the time; guys were still covering their bikes with loads and loads of Bondo molding, and I wanted to focus on something different.

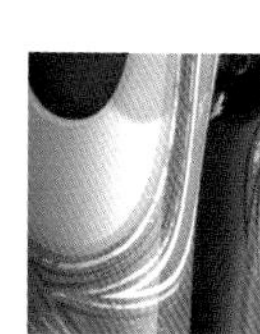

Basically, to do the leafwork I would have my brother busy prepping all the bare steel for the paint jobs. Then I'd paint the bodywork and the frames, and two guys that I worked with who were really talented—Roy Mason and John Harnett—would come in and lay down the gold leaf. They had to work with the precision of surgeons, because laying down these designs involved working with a soft material that was paper thin and came in 4x4-inch sheets. It was so delicate it would crumble in your hands if you handled it the wrong way. I'd paint the surface in advance with special glue and lay the leaf over it, then lay several clear coats on top of that.

A good 10 years before TV would make him a household name, Dave was building one-off custom bikes for professional wrestler Hulk Hogan.

There were a few other guys working with gold leaf back then, like Arlen Ness, but the process tended to make the bikes really expensive to finish and, unlike today, there still wasn't a whole lot of money to be made building spendy choppers and custom bikes. It was tough to even turn a buck on the really elaborate bikes in which I'd invested all my creativity and months of labor.

People ask me all the time why I did so many Hondas back then. They were actually a fairly smart investment. My brother had one to ride, and we liked Hondas because they were cheap, reliable, and you could beat the shit out of them—something you couldn't always get away with on an American Twin. We'd buy a CB 750 for a few hundred dollars, customize it, ride the hell out of it, and still wouldn't lose much money when we sold it. So without much money pouring in from building ground-up show bikes, I used to paint a lot of bikes for the other builders. At the time only a few guys really did their own custom painting, so we had an area of expertise that really paid off.

When I think back to those days, it's funny that I never would have guessed how it could become what it is now. During my early career, I never even

A Ness tail-dragger fender, apehangers, and a set of funky organ exhausts drew stares for this Perewitz original.

considered how big it could get. I was just plugging along, painting other builders' bikes, building two or three of my own bikes each year, and just doing my thing, never expecting anything to come of it besides what we'd already achieved: a reasonably successful business doing something I loved. I was raising a family, had plenty of good friends to ride with, and had plenty of recognition at the shows every year, so I guess I was satisfied. But slowly, over the 1980s, things got better for us at Cycle Fab, ultimately due to all the hard work and long hours I'd put in.

A lot of times back then, instead of just buying something new for a bike, a guy would bring his beat-up motorcycle into Cycle Fab and we'd end up working on the one he already had, like putting a new front section or rear end on his stock frame, or stretching and painting his existing gas tank, or cutting his fenders. Guys today have a lot more money to spend (and a lot more aftermarket specialties to choose from) so they just go out and buy new stuff, and a lot of perfectly good parts end up getting thrown away.

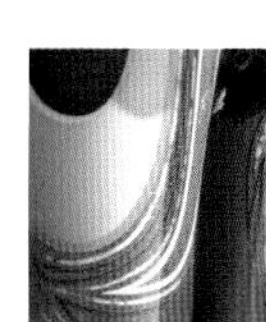

With a mouth that breathed actual fire, the Dragonman chopper was one of the East Coast's most famous customized bikes.

Beautiful finishes and some serious rake on this late-model Perewitz Cycle Fab stretch chopper.

Occasionally I see bikes I built real early on, but very rarely. That's a surprise, because so many of the guys I sold bikes to still live in the area. Unfortunately, people give up riding for whatever reason, and the bikes, a lot of them, are just stuck sitting in somebody's garage collecting dust. I'd really love to buy some of them back if I had the chance. I'd love to see how the work's held up.

I did have a chance to do just that, not too long ago, when the wife of an old customer called and said, "He's got a bike you built in 1978 if you want to come see it." I remembered exactly what it was. I was really excited and made arrangements to go see it, traveling to his place about 50 miles away. I'd brought cash and planned to bring the bike back home with me, but when I got there, it was a huge disappointment. It was *awful.* In fact, it was in such rough shape that it would have cost me more to restore it than to build a completely new one from scratch. There was rust and corrosion on all the chrome parts, and the paint had discolored badly—even the motor was beat. That's too bad, because a man doesn't get too many chances to own something like that in his lifetime.

There wasn't anybody asking for my autograph back then. When people came to the shop, they didn't come just to take pictures to prove they were there. They were usually riders who had heard about us from some fellow rider and came needing work done on their bikes. Even today, with my other media and marketing appearances, the magazines are still a great way to reach people. They

continued on page 79

Opposite page: **The business end of a Perewitz chopper.**

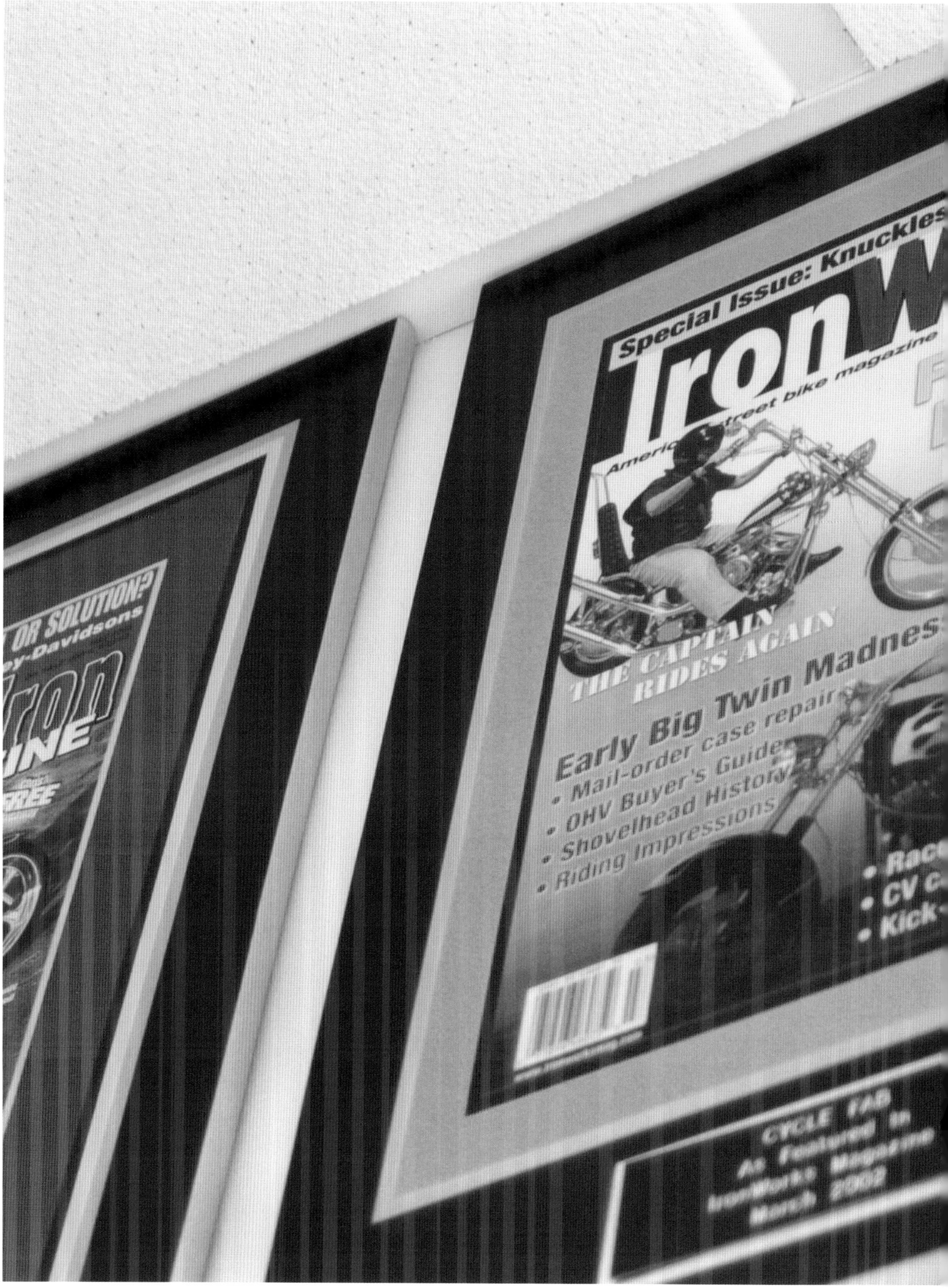
OR SOLUTION?
-Davidsons
Special Issue: Knuckles
Iron
street bike magazine
THE CAPTAIN
RIDES AGAIN
Early Big Twin Madnes
• Mail-order case repair
• OHV Buyer's Guide
• Shovelhead History
• Riding Impressions
CYCLE FAB
As Featured in
IronWorks Magazine
March 2002

By the second decade of business Cycle Fab's work was appearing regularly on magazine covers.

Opposite page and below: **Twin downdraft carbs and an engraved motor provide eye candy on the Magna Cycle, but where's the top frame rail?**

play an important part in publicizing what we do. We understand this completely, because when someone calls from, say, some out-of-the-way foreign place like Tasmania, Australia, you can guess where people get your name—most often from the magazine articles.

Harley-Davidson motors were extremely unreliable back then. We did what we could to make the best of it, because everybody knew that if you wanted to be cool, you rode a Harley. But the American Twins were plagued with all sorts of motor and transmission problems, and because I came from a background where I'd almost exclusively used Sportster powerplants, I had somehow gotten used to them detonating, breaking engine cases, and having bottom-end problems from time to time.

I know that when you look at all the old *Easyriders* magazines, you always see guys building choppers out of old Knuckleheads and Panheads, but that was more of a West Coast thing. The antique customs really weren't much of a trend around New England. None of the guys I hung out with had old bikes, and when you saw one, it was usually a restoration job at an antique bike show and not a chopped-out flame job. We didn't really embrace the new Evolution engine when it came out in the mid-1980s, even though we'd heard there were huge improvements to reliability and performance. Basically, the Evolutions were way

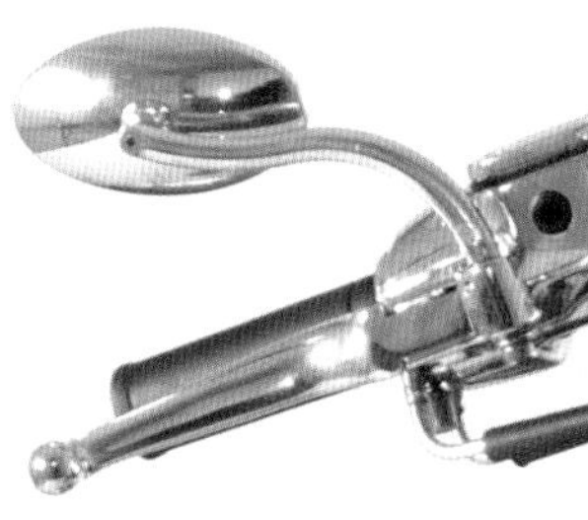

Who says dressers have to look boring? This Softail received the full flame treatment. "I like a bike that looks great but you can still ride it a long distance. If you can't ride 'em, what's the use? This bike is owned by my friend Bob Belanger, aka Be Bop."

Joe Pro, another satisfied Cycle Fab customer, on his pride and joy. This is Joe's 15th Perewitz bike.

too pricey to use in a custom project. You could still pick up a Shovelhead or Ironhead Sportster engine as a basket case for a few hundred bucks, but the new Evolution engine was kind of an unknown thing, and it was expensive, so it was several years before you started seeing them in custom bikes.

The number one thing all bike builders need is good, hard experience: that will be more important than anything else during your career. Like I said, the big chopper and custom parts aftermarket didn't get started until the early 1980s, but I'd already been at it since the late 1960s and had learned most of the tricks of the trade by the 1980s. I didn't need to rely on catalog orders as much as some other builders. I had a background in working with sheet metal from my years in the body shop and I knew how to paint. I'd been welding long enough to know about frames and raking the front ends. In addition to that, I'd worked in a couple of machine shops as a kid along the way, too, so my shop could cover just about everything onsite. There were no problems we couldn't get through there, and it's all because our years of experience in parts fabrication. Even nowadays, when you can pretty much buy a chopper in a box and bolt it together, to do it right it's still essential to know metalsmith skills so you can bail yourself out if you run into a problem. Unfortunately, there are very few young builders who have had the time to acquire all those skills.

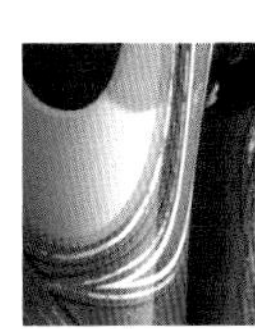

Opposite page: **What a long, strange trip it's been—psychedelic paint swirls across this tank bring back memories.**

Long, low, and powerful, Dave prefers the pro-street style for its performance advantages over other bikes.

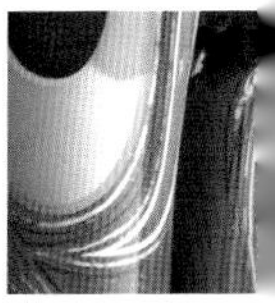

Above: A collection of previous Cycle Fabrications signs, dating from 1975 to 2004, on display in the latest shop.

Left: Timeless cool is captured in this classic, 1950s-style bobber custom built by Cycle Fab's chief fabricator Big Ron Landers.

By the end of the 1980s, we had probably built 100 bikes and custom-painted maybe three times that many. I had hit Daytona, and Laconia every year since 1970, and I would always compare my work to other builders'. Back then we all knew each other, and when we'd size up a custom bike, we'd almost always know right away who had built it. Arlen, Donnie, and I would usually have some of the best bikes. There'd be a small group of us at the big Rat's Hole show, and pretty much every year it was one of us who built the winning bike.

Even by the late 1980s it was still a very small group. We didn't have much knowledge of the European scene because we didn't see the foreign builders at the shows. There wasn't this modern kind of open competition between builders to be the most famous or to see who could sell their bikes for the most money. With our group, even after we'd spent all winter building new bikes to compete against each other at the Daytona show, we'd still all go out together later to grab a beer and talk shop. Everybody was open with each other about what techniques

continued on page 95

The fruits of four decades in the chopper-building industry include some seriously dedicated fans!

When he's not welding, machining, or fabricating parts, Kory Souza gets to take a ride on one of the radical stretch choppers that he builds and designs.

Top: **The Hamster's Fall Foliage run charity auction on Cape Cod.**

Bottom: **The group started as a joke among a crew that included Arlen Ness, Donnie Smith, and Dave Perewitz; today, there are hundreds of Hamsters in several countries.**

Boomerang Honda

Keeping afloat in the custom motorcycle game for the better part of four decades means witnessing more than your share of trends, change, and recurring design themes among bike fans. For Dave Perewitz and the Cycle Fab crew, staying the course means occasionally getting the feeling that you've seen a motorcycle before . . . and more than just once. Such is the case with this deep blue Honda CB 750, a motorcycle that Dave has customized no fewer than six times over the course of his career. Purchased new in 1970 by Bill Twiss, one of Dave's oldest friends, the Honda was actually one of Perewitz's better-known custom show bikes after it appeared in the pages of *Street Chopper* magazine in the early 1980s.

Painted a vivid yellow back then and adorned with a 150-mm (4-inch) rear bias-ply tire, the Honda was something of a rolling advertisement for Cycle Fab's work. Dave remembers trying out several different aftermarket parts on the bike before settling on a set of modified stock fenders painted to match the frame. Though shapelier aftermarket options were available, the stock Honda breadbox gas tank stayed in place because, at a 5-plus-gallon capacity, it offered all-day fun between refueling, an unfathomable option on most choppers.

The motor, always the Japanese bike's strong point, received an 836-cc big bore kit, complete with high-lift cams, flat slide Mikuni carburetors, and copious amounts of chrome.

Bill Twiss' Honda uses a Ceriani front end.

This blue Honda CB750 appeared in the pages of *Street Chopper* in 1980 and has been reworked several times in the past 30 years. It's hit the streets as a stretch chopper, a digger, and everything in between.

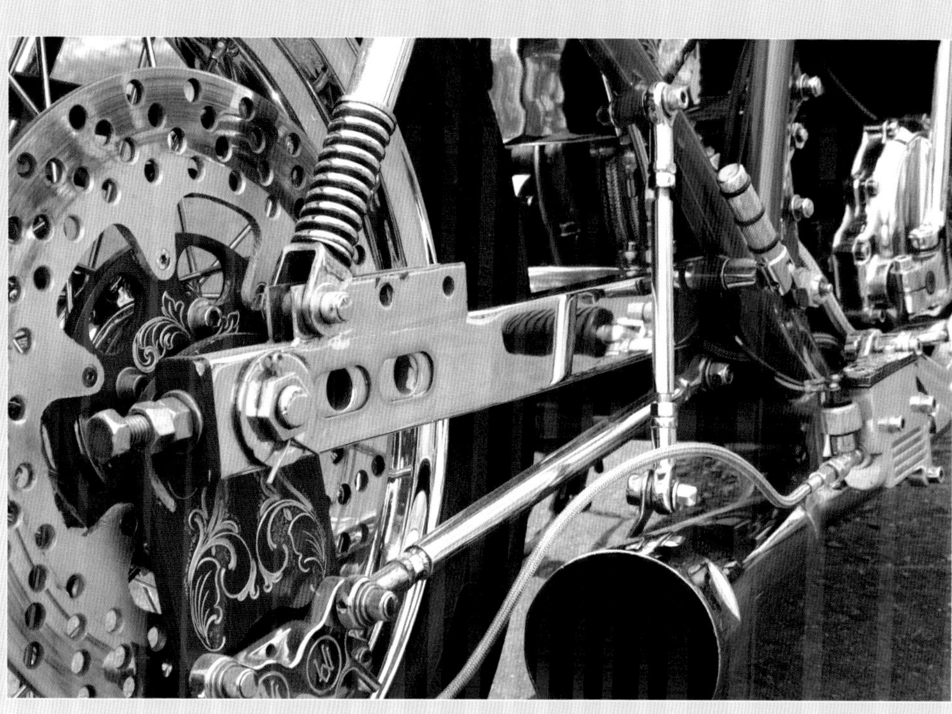

The Hondas, with their smooth-running overhead cam four-cylinder engines, were perfect test beds for the then-burgeoning import chopper field, and over its long life this one has been adorned with a garageful of custom parts.

Today, the bike has had its rear shocks replaced with a set of Donnie Smith's semi-rigid struts, a modification that lowers the tall, sport-touring bike's riding position while helping to show off the chromed rear-wheel spokes. To accommodate the wider rear wheel, the stock Honda swingarm has been cut and widened before being welded back together. The original steep steering angle is more relaxed today, thanks to a weld-on top rail and neck that kick out the steering an additional few degrees.

The owner, who Dave says stops by nearly every day to contemplate another makeover for his 36-year-old street bike, has decided to go with a more sedate dark blue finish after years of dazzling paint jobs that could be seen coming for miles. Though custom parts for the old Honda fours are getting thin on the ground after four decades, Dave says he welcomes the challenge of rebuilding and redesigning the Honda as many times as the owner likes. "It's always a challenge to come up with something new and different after you've worked on a motorcycle so many times, but whatever we come up with, Bill tends to like it," he said.

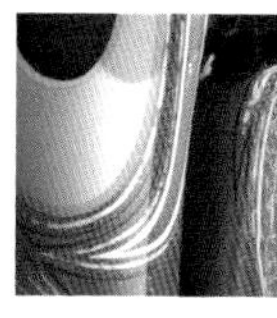

Opposite page: **Looking like an updated version of the motorcycles a young Dave Perewitz idolized as a teen, this funky, post-modern bobber re-creates custom bike history.**

Below: **Whether he's painting an oil tank or a tiny handlebar cover, Cycle Fab spray wizard Jay Crone always brings his best game.**

they were using and who was supplying them with the best parts. If one of us ran into a problem building something, we could always call each other, or sometimes even ask somebody to fly in and help out. Sharing all kinds of information like that really doesn't go on anymore, except among us old-school guys who've been working together for 30 years now.

Though I did lots of bodywork and frame modifications over the years, I only built my own chassis components for a short time. It was something I'd seen myself doing for years, and I knew I had the ability, but in the end the profit margin was too small for the amount of work involved. The guy who manufactured chassis for us was a top sprint-car chassis builder, who did first-class car stuff, but he just could not get the bike frame down, even after several tries. Try as he might, he could never get them to ride perfectly. We experimented a while with this Softail-style design, but on frame after frame it never worked out to our satisfaction.

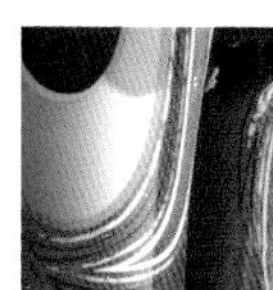

continued on page 101

This Rigid old-style chopper belongs to friend and fellow Hamster, Bob Belanger.

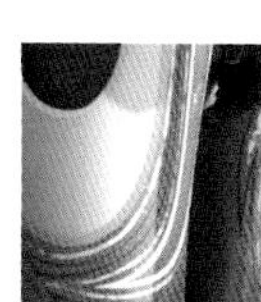

"They never show you on TV just how much work goes into finishing a motorcycle. You just can't rush it."

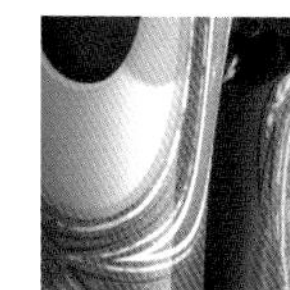

Armed with a photographic memory, Dave usually concocts the ideas for rides, like this badass yellow chop, in his head. From there, each member of the team brings ideas and tricks to the table until a thing of beauty is produced.

Eventually, I just went back to using frames from other builders. And I don't have any regrets about that, because sometimes builders will get too caught up in trying to do everything themselves. In reality, most builders would serve themselves and their customers better by just sticking with what they know best. I have no problem using a good chassis or a set of forks from a talented builder. Joey Perse makes some incredible front ends that are really high quality, and I'm proud to have his stuff on my bikes. Same goes for the frames that Eddie Trotta makes: they're strong enough for these huge motors people crave today, and they look really good.

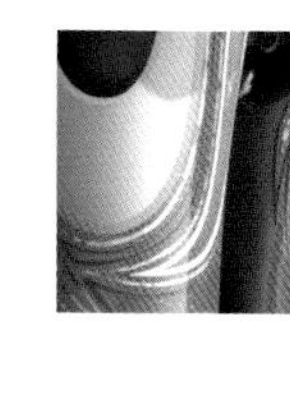

NIVER

Joe Pro's pro-street-style bike gets ridden daily.

Chapter Three

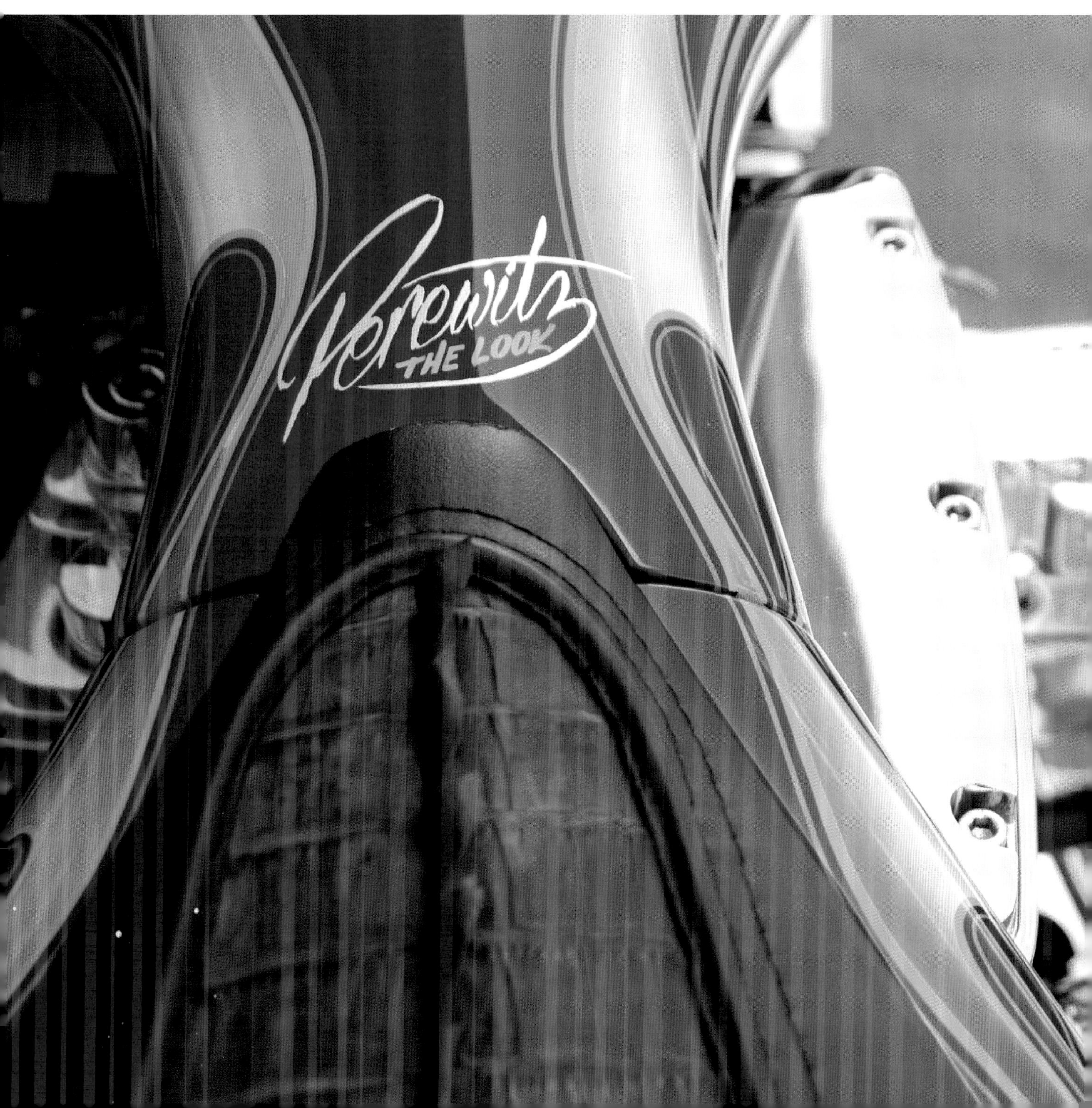

Big Bikes, Bigger Bucks

Above: **What could be cooler than grabbing a cold one from a custom-painted fridge?**

Left: **The alligator who gave up his hide for this chopper's saddle couldn't have asked for a more interesting afterlife!**

GARELICK FARMS
SPRAY
LUBRICANT

By the time 1990 rolled around, I was giving the business 100 percent. I kind of got back into it very heavily once the kids were old enough to look after themselves.

Currently, all three kids work in the business, which is something I never planned on. Kids have minds of their own, and my son Jesse is a perfect example of this. He's had his own business repairing small engines and keeping lawn mowers and tractors running for friends of the family and neighbors, since he was maybe 11 years old. He even took over the backyard shed, just as I had done, and had his own little business out there. I can't take credit for his interest in small-engine repair, because I didn't know the first thing about lawn mowers even though I'd worked as a mechanic for years. As my father didn't about motorcycles.

One day Jesse just started playing around with them, and the next thing you know, he's repairing lawn equipment for neighbors and some of his junior high–school teachers. I never leaned on him to follow me into the motorcycle business, but Jesse started working at an engine repair shop, Pro Equipment, all by himself. And now, 15 years later, he's an unbelievable technician and invaluable in the shop. He's got this skill for troubleshooting problems of every imaginable kind, using theory to attack an issue whether it's a car, truck, motorcycle, or lawnmower.

Opposite page: **Many chefs help make the Cycle Fab stew, with each member of the team contributing ideas to the mix.**

Dave transformed this 2003 anniversary Fat Boy into a pro-street custom for Aerosmith's Brad Whitford.

Though his career as a custom vehicle designer began in a Chevrolet repair shop, the Perewitz look has ascended into true art. Flames are hand-laid in the old-school style, and then individually airbrushed to perfection.

Jesse has experienced every aspect of bike building and he's essential and efficient when it comes to scheduling, handling details, and running the parts department. When it comes right down to it, he's worked in service pretty much forever, and once, when one of the mechanics was injured on the job, Jesse pulled four weeks as a welder. I guess a part of this comes with having been around it all his life. It's left him unafraid to try new things and even tackle difficult jobs that might scare off some other young guys. Naturally, I try to encourage things like that, but I wouldn't press him if he didn't want to work in the shop.

By the early 1990s, things continued to change technologically, with more efficient disc brakes on all the bikes, very few kick-starters in use, and components that were better made and more expensive. There were materials, like billet aluminum, coming in that we couldn't have imagined 20 years earlier. There was rubber mounting for the engines, which made the bikes a lot smoother and easier to ride than they were just a few years earlier. Instead of these thick, fat, 16-inch bias-ply monsters on the wire Hog wheels, people started mounting low-profile radials that were low and wide, like the tires on an imported crotch rocket. The motorcycles started to get more expensive, too, both to build and to sell when it came time, but it was just about the time that wealthy people started to become bikers—let's call them the high-profile type of customer. They saw what they were missing out on. These were people who had enough money that it really didn't matter how much something cost: they were willing to pay it in order to have something well crafted and one of a kind.

Never a fan of overly long front ends, Dave prefers a custom motorcycle that handles as sharp as it looks.

About this time, I'd built a really cool bike with an Arlen Ness swingarm frame, rubber mounting for the engine. My good friend Wayne Loftain, also known as Tattoo Wayne, built an Evolution Big Twin with two front heads instead of the traditional front-and-rear cylinder setup. We managed this by moving the intake ports to the left side of the engine and welding the original ports shut. We had a carb coming out of each side and it was really trick-looking.

My friend Wayne is a serious speed freak who went from a gas bike to a pro-street bike and, eventually, ran in the top-fuel class in drag racing for 12 to 15 years. I was involved with some of that adventure: helping him keep those drag bikes together, building parts when he needed them, and occasionally painting one of his race bikes. Wayne had maybe 18 national drag-racing records, but he still insisted on building his own motors and fabricating all the frames for his bikes himself.

Anyway, I remember the dual-carb bike had the very first set of billet wheels any of us had seen on the street. They were made by Sandy Kossman, who makes drag-racing stuff; Sandy made the wheels especially for me. I ended up selling that bike in 1990 for $20,000, and though that may not seem like

Notice the detail of the metalflake incorporated into the deep-green paint job on the oil tank—nice!

much money for a custom bike today, at the time I was the talk of the industry for getting that much cash for one bike. At the shows people would be saying, "Did you hear that Perewitz got 20 grand for that bike?" Amazed as they were, I had easily put that much into the bike just in parts while I was building it!

It wasn't until a few years later that the whole industry started to change and pricing went through the roof. And the funny thing is, when the bikes first started getting more expensive, I still sold to the same clientele for a while. These were just the same guys who had been coming around forever, guys who either wanted one of my bikes or came to see me because they liked what I did and wanted me to paint and customize bikes they already owned.

When bikes started costing more to build and sell, I thought there was nothing better than to be in a position where I could build cool shit and get paid for it. I had plenty of new ideas and techniques I'd been itching to try out, and the money was finally coming in, which gave me a chance to experiment like I

Narrow at the waist and wide at the ends, late-model Cycle Fab bikes are built for comfort and looks.

Known for his low-slung
pro-street roadsters,
this green Perewitz beauty
encompasses five
decades of custom
motorcycle craftsmanship.

never had before. People forget how long we did this for no money. I once built a totally customized Honda CB 750 back in 1977, and it was a full-scale custom bike. It had hand-built parts, a rigid frame, hand-built fenders, and a one-of-a-kind gas tank. I even took the time to rework the handlebars. After all that work and all that sweat, I remember giving the guy the bill for construction, paint, parts, and everything. I had bought it all and built it by hand, and the tab was 6 grand. That's all. By today's standards, it was easily an $80,000 bike.

But I don't think I was alone here. I don't think any of us were making any money then. It was a tough business. Over the years, working such long hours for not a lot of money could definitely take its toll. Fortunately, I had gotten married in 1979 and moved to Bridgewater, Massachusetts, out in the woods with no neighbors to bother us, which made it possible to keep my sanity all those years. And things were about to become very different.

By the 1990s, when people's tastes were changing from narrow, skinny choppers to more billet and Fat Bob bikes, there ended up being a lot more paintwork to do. I was still painting as many bikes as I had in the 1980s, but the jobs got bigger; the average bike went from three or four pieces, to five or six pieces that all needed painting. Paint quality had improved, and you could do so much more with it that paint was actually replacing a lot of chrome on the custom motorcycles I was doing. Instead of chroming the lower fork legs, wheels,

Hamsters memorabilia turns up at the shop from members around the world.

and air cleaner, people wanted that stuff painted, which was a lot of work.

We started using urethane-based paints, and it was tough making that transition. I hated the urethane paints because I'd been working with lacquer my whole life. I had reached a point where I knew how to fix little mistakes and major screw-ups fairly easily, and then, all of a sudden, everything changed. It was a whole new learning curve. It was especially tough going through all the technical transitions: the products kept evolving, all the paint guns changed, even the amount of air pressure they needed to operate was suddenly different.

We spent a lot of time just figuring out the basics all over again. It's funny how trends in custom biking changed without us noticing it at first. It was the same familiar game for many years, then all of a sudden, wild graphics took over for the gold leaf and people wanted different styles, like skulls and flames and all sorts of trendy, tribal designs on their bodywork. At any rate, our motorcycles were still appearing in a lot of magazines, so we were steadily getting more popular.

My paint business had grown so much that I needed reliable help. I couldn't find just anyone to do the custom paint jobs we were doing. It had to be someone with skill and technique. Keith Hanson started to work with me, doing custom paint jobs. He definitely had the skills and techniques. He did a great job, was always reliable, and told me where we were at. Working as a team, we always made deadlines. Keith and I are still a team: we work on jobs together daily. We have become great friends over the years.

One of the biggest changes—and one of the biggest improvements in the past couple of decades—has been the emergence of the big-inch motors. There

This interesting collection of Cycle Fab machinery displays the shop's varied customizing styles, with everything from baggers to choppers. This photo was taken during the Hamster's Fall Foliage run at Cape Cod.

A Softail chopper awaits its first ride from a happy customer. Dig the scramble of exhaust headers and the tiny gap between fender and wheel.

Although dozens of manufacturers have offered their products his way, Dave prefers to build his bikes around the strong, reliable Total Performance motor.

are a whole lot of excellent motors on the market these days. They're just incredible as far as power and reliability go, and have come very far in a very short period of time. For example: I recall a guy who came in with a 96-ci motor in his Harley Softail in the early 1990s, and it was nothing but trouble. It would never start, had problems with the rings, and it was just a fucker to try to ride on the street every day.

But today, a 96-ci engine is almost considered a baby motor by comparison. Everything's well over 100 ci, they're more powerful, and they're more reliable. Everything from the air induction systems to fuel delivery to suspension components have been improved, so you don't have to worry about a big motor shaking itself to pieces like some of the old stroker mills did back in the 1970s. There are excellent motors on the market these days. I started working with Tom from TP Engineering about 15 years ago, and I've never looked back. I get a lot of offers to use different engines and a lot of it I could probably get for free because of the TV exposure or because they want the business I've been getting, but I won't take it unless I can make it work.

Customers are more likely to find a rusty spoke than an empty work lift at Cycle Fab.

The same goes for Bert Baker of Baker Drivetrain. I've been with him ever since he began and he's got great products that hold up over time in all sorts of conditions, so I'll always use his transmissions. When right-side-drive transmissions came along, we worked with Bert and Phil Day of Daytec Frames to build a right-side frame to accept the new Avon 250 tire and Bert's right-side transmission. He was the first one to make right-side drives that worked with the wider rear tires, so you didn't have to offset the motors. This was important for guys running with 250- and 300-mm tires, because with the stock left-side transmission and the heavy left-hand offset, the bikes want to fall over to the left all the time.

Even though I know better, I'm still always surprised to see the lack of craftsmanship on some of the custom bikes that roll into my shop today. Some of these motorcycles are built by top-flight builders for big money, but when they come in, we can't believe some of the serious defects these people will just cover up with Bondo. A bike came in recently and part of the frame rail had been undercut and built up with Bondo, which was totally unsafe. We have seen parts that may have split from vibration or hard use, where it was just obvious that they were not meant to fit together in any kind of way; they're just forced together and puttied over.

In 1993 I built a motorcycle for Hulk Hogan—a bike he actually rode in a movie—and another one for a wrestler named Brutus Beefcake. Hulk Hogan was referred to me by Tony Carlini, a West Coast builder who originally came from Detroit. Tony was working in L.A. and involved with movie stars. He had a

Although the 12-inch rim width of this billet aluminum rear wheel does little to help this motorcycle around corners, it does look damn cool.

Top: Designing new exhaust headers is a time-consuming business; they not only have to look good, but they also have to run strong as well.

Bottom: The group ID is displayed proudly on this chopper.

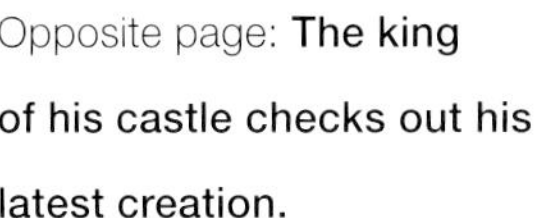

Opposite page: The king of his castle checks out his latest creation.

Ferrari dealership and he knew Hulk Hogan, who asked for a guy who could build him the kind of custom bike he wanted. Tony recommended me. It was the first bike I'd built for a guy of that size, and we had to stretch the frame to suit him because he's so tall. We actually had him come in and fitted him to the bike, making all sorts of adjustments so he'd be comfortable riding down the road.

That job led to all kinds of other high-profile work, including five bikes I built for Ruben Brown, who played guard for the Buffalo Bills and Chicago Bears. Ruben called me out of the blue one day and asked me to build him a bike. Right now I'm in the process of finishing my sixth bike for him. What makes him really great is that he likes all kinds of bikes, starting off with a customized Road King, followed by a smaller, stretched pro-street bike, and then a chopper. Later on, we worked together on a couple of charity events and he had me build him a Road Glide. Now I'm doing a skinny, antique-style bike for him. Ruben's a serious biker who rides every day he can, even though the NFL doesn't like it. Ruben is a great rider and a good friend. We get together several times a year and ride together, and he knows what he's doing out there.

Every now and then, somebody calls me up and asks to buy a bike. That's a hard question, because I don't tend to have a lot of bikes for sale. Everything is pretty much pre-sold, so the only bike I ever have for sale are the ones I build for

continued on page 130

Let the Motorcycle Do the Talkin' or Singin'

Though he's not much of a fan of the high-concept custom motorcycles that attempt to make a rigid chopper resemble, say, a Good Humor ice cream truck from the 1950s or a Phantom jet, one of Dave Perewitz's best-known custom bikes is actually concept-driven. The bold yellow chopper he built in 2002 in honor of New England's greatest rock band has brought Cycle Fabrications more time in the spotlight than probably any of its other creations.

The Aerosmith chopper that Perewitz completed in 2004 was a labor of love, conducted at the request of Minnesota native Drew Donnelley. The banker and longtime Aerosmith fan also had a soft spot for custom motorcycles, and had visited Cycle Fab on several occasions to talk about having a chopper built. It was only after discussing plans to build a bike that Dave inadvertently let on that he had recently built a bike for Aerosmith guitarist Brad Whitford, and invited Donnelley to come along to Whitford's place for a visit.

"This guy is probably like the world's biggest Aerosmith fan; he's seen them I don't know how many dozens of times, and has parts of his house decorated with band memorabilia. When we got to Brad's house and I introduced them, Drew was like a star-struck little kid. He said it was the greatest day of his life, and it was so cool when later he got to know the guys in the band and they all became friends," Dave said.

Not only did the band form a friendship with their biggest fan, the meeting also inspired longtime Cycle Fab painter Keith Hanson to create a series of murals on a chopper that the shop was preparing for Donnelley. The bike ended up spurring the imaginations of the entire Cycle Fab crew as it came together to build a 120-horsepower tribute to the band.

Among the more stunning custom accents are a set of actual microphones—once used on stage by singer Steven Tyler, of course—set up for use as handlebar grips, and they hold up as well on the road as they did in concert. The bike is built around a Daytec Softail chassis, running a massive 63-mm Spike inverted front end with Performance Machine wheels and disc brakes. The Russ Wernimont fenders and Cycle Fab fuel tank are recipients of the Hanson murals of the band members, as is the Daytec oil tank.

As with many late-model Perewitz customs, this machine transfers power to the gearbox with a Baker six-speed transmission, utilizing a right-side drive for perfect balance. Cranked up and running, the Aerosmith chopper is as loud as a stage full of Marshall amplifiers set to maximum romp, thanks to the tried-and-true Cycle Fab combination of a big-inch TP Engineering engine—this one bumping 121 cubes of polished billet aluminum good for around 120 horsepower at the rear axle—and a set of TCX custom open pipes. Twin Mikuni side-draft carburetors drag in enough wind to fill a sail, while a solo seat by Danny Gray bears the title "Back in the Saddle," one of the band's best-known hit songs.

If there had ever been any doubt how much the band members appreciated seeing themselves immortalized by their favorite custom motorcycle builder, it instantly evaporated when the Aerosmith crew saw the machine for the first time. I don't think I've ever seen so many really famous guys all completely speechless, all at the same time. To date, this awesome bike has been featured onstage at several concerts and Dave says that singer Steven Tyler, who has ridden the bike more than once, has repeatedly asked the owner to sell. "I don't think he ever would. Not this guy," Dave laughs.

Top: **An actual microphone used by Aerosmith singer Steven Tyler is now a bar-end weight.**

Left: **The Aerosmith chopper was built for a fan and features some of the finest detailing of any Cycle Fabrications bike.**

AEROSMITH

Built around a Daytec pro-street Softail-style chassis, the machine is powered by a 100-horsepower TP engine.

Aerosmith guitarist Brad Whitford owns several Perewitz customs.

Cycle Fab's resident paint wizard Keith Hanson detailed the machine to precision.

Guitarist Joe Perry, immortalized in motorcycle art.

A massive flying eye decoration overlooking the workshop at Cycle Fab, where you're just as likely to find folks doing business as hanging out.

myself, which is maybe once or twice a year. As custom bikes grew in popularity, it was sometime around the year 2000 that we had the big switch in clientele from the traditional chopper guys and hardcore bikers we were used to. That's when we started seeing the kind of folks who weren't really even bikers, but celebrities and such. I had done a little celebrity work previously, but the jobs were few and far between. Back then, I don't think a lot of stars were allowed by their managers or contracts to ride motorcycles because people were worried they'd get hurt.

The projects I've been involved in that people ask me about the most are the Aerosmith bikes. They came about because a TV show, called *Steel Dreams*, with Aerosmith guitarist Brad Whitford focused on the motorcycle industry and people who rode and built bikes. Brad is a guy who loves cool stuff. He has a collection of muscle cars and now bikes. Brad says that if he wasn't a musician he would be racing cars somewhere. He's a really cool, down-to-earth guy and we became friends while I put a bike together for him a few years ago. Brad appreciates all kinds of custom bikes, from baggers to choppers and everything in between, so we really have a good time designing stuff for him.

Members of the band live very close to my shop and they stop over from time to time when they're not on the road. Steven Tyler is a new bike enthusiast who just started riding a couple of years back. Turns out he's really passionate

about it and is one of those people who wishes he'd found motorcycling earlier in his life.

The *Steel Dreams* program first aired here in New England, and pretty soon it was all over the country. Thinking back to the years when custom bikes were pretty much underground, it was wild to see a whole TV show about me, painting bikes and riding and hanging out with Brad. I really enjoy it and have never found the TV crews to be a problem; they're just more people hanging around the shop, talking bikes. Host Ralph Sheehan got one of my flame jobs on his custom Softail. I make it a special point to always sign autographs for people when they recognize me. More than anything, I think it's very important to remember that, even though you're on TV, you can still be the same person you always have been, and you're no different—or better—than anyone else.

By the late 1990s, there were more people building custom motorcycles than ever before, but still not as many as you see today. You could still ride your bike someplace and the average person who didn't know anything about motorcycles wouldn't even notice it, unlike today. By this time, we still had just three or four people working in the building at any one time, and we were only able to do

Where his motorcycles were once judged at bike shows, Dave is more likely to be found these days judging the work of others.

maybe four or five custom bike projects a year, tops. As things progressed into the late 1990s, the whole nature of the business started to change, and I was glad I'd had the time to raise my kids before everything really heated up. By then, we were doing an awful lot of traveling. Last year, for example, I was only home three weekends from January to November, and it was tough, let me tell you. But on the other hand, the money is definitely a lot better than it ever was.

When there is an upcoming event, being a small shop we're under incredible pressure, working almost around the clock for weeks on end. We don't end up getting much sleep and are just so relieved when the whole thing is finished. And it always—always—takes longer than you expect it to. No matter how well you've planned or how many parts you have in advance, these bikes take a long time and a lot of effort to produce.

Sometimes it pisses me off that custom motorcycles on TV can be built from the floor up in just one day's time. I know from decades of experience that it's physically not possible. I'm aware that TV is TV and it's all make-believe, anyway, and with a fully set-up shop capable of everything, it is *possible* to build a motorcycle fairly quickly. But I also know there's lots of planning and mistakes

The private entrance to Dave's office.

Completed customs for sale in the Bridgewater showroom sell briskly all though the year, according to Dave.

Most of the bikes on display at our shop are customer's bikes. If there are 20 bikes on the floor, there might be three for sale.

and the inevitable things you'll find that unexpectedly need fabricating in order to do a complete job and end up with a safe, rideable motorcycle.

As much as things have changed in some respects, building custom motorcycles still hasn't been all that different than it always has been. For each of the big events in a given year, we still are expected to show up with a completely new bike. This has been particularly important for Sturgis, even back when I first started, and still is because it is guaranteed that most of the custom bike magazines will be at Sturgis, so you have to have your hottest, newest bike there and ready to go.

The custom bike industry has always been big California for as long as anybody can remember, but I never once thought of relocating out there. Yeah, I know that they have the really pretty weather, but it's always been funny to talk with Arlen Ness on the phone when I'm buried in 2 feet of snow, he's sweating in 80-degree heat, and I've got no chance of even getting out on a short ride anytime

Left: **Even Dave's business-card holder is flamed.**

Opposite page: **Painted hard parts like these orange-sprayed handlebars make all the difference between show-winners and also-rans.**

in the next three months. But the Northeast is my home, always has been, and this is where I want to stay—nowhere else. Plus, these really long, snowy winters up here give us plenty of time to work on bikes and try out new ideas.

Even though many things have changed, after all these years, going to an event like Sturgis and attending the big custom bike shows is still a lot of fun. Not only because you get to meet the general public, but you also want your friends in the industry to see what you've done and you want to catch up with all the guys you've been too busy to see for a while. And while I love the shows, to be honest, I was never after trophies. I actually haven't had a bike in a show since the early 1980s. I don't enter the shows because I feel it's really just not the right thing to do at my level. I don't want to compete against my customers. A guy once asked me while I was building him a high-dollar bike if I could guarantee that he'd be a winner at shows. I told him, "Don't put your bike in competition, put it in Display only and you will always come out a winner."

Rockin' Ride

Chapter Four

Cycle Fabulous

Above: **"When TV crews show up, we just have to remember to keep working like nothing's happening." (Dave Perewitz)**

Left: **This rigid-framed chopper was Dave's shop bike for a while. Whenever they needed an extra bike for a ride it was pressed into duty.**

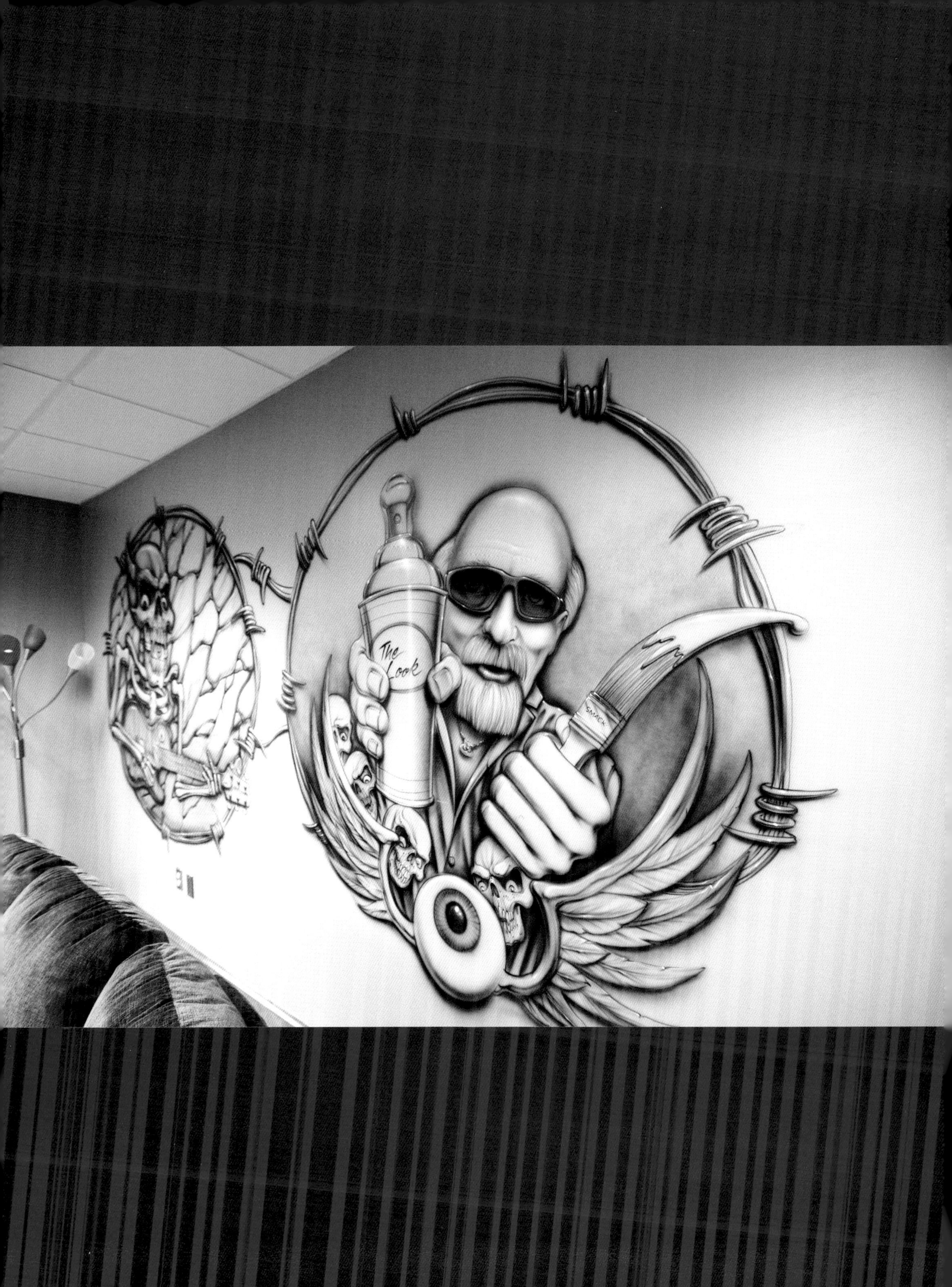
The Look
SMACK

Entering the year 2000, things were starting to happen for me in a big way. For one, it was the third year I'd received an invitation to take part in the Camel Roadhouse promotion by the R. J. Reynolds Tobacco Company. This was the biggest, most widely recognized custom motorcycle promotion going on in the country at the time, and there were some really special people involved with the tour. I was thrilled just to be a part of it.

What made it such a great deal was that Camel not only paid us to build bikes, but also transported the motorcycles around the country to all these big rallies put on by the company. This meant that all sorts of people saw my work who might not have ever been aware of it otherwise. It was also truly a cool experience to meet and work beside a lot of the better younger builders, and hang out with the guys I'd known for a long time, too, like Ron Simms. The Camel tours reminded me that even though the custom bike business was getting a lot more competitive and there was far more money involved, we could all still have a lot of fun when we got together, hanging out with really talented builders.

I'd been friends with Jesse James from West Coast Choppers for a long time. I knew Jesse even before he was doing much with custom bikes, back when he'd been working at Performance Machine and, later, for hot rod builder Boyd Coddington. While he was at Boyd, Jesse had designed billet wheels for some of

Opposite page: **A piece of original airbrushed wall art—a portrait of Dave by Mike Learn—adorns one of the shop's walls. Art and artifacts like these keep a steady line of customers passing through the doors.**

the bikes we'd built at Cycle Fab, so he had always been somebody I considered a friend.

Well, Jesse must have felt the same way, and has always been a really good guy, so he called me one day and told me about a show the Discovery Channel had just proposed to do about him and his shop out in Long Beach. They were going to call it *Motorcycle Mania*. It would be directed by Hugh King from Original Productions, a TV production studio out of California. Jesse was cool enough to call and let me know they would be filming at Daytona that year, which meant I ended up meeting the whole crew and making an appearance on the show. That was my first real exposure on television, and it was pretty cool, but even cooler was the fact that it started me down the road to other TV specials.

So I should give credit to Jesse James, who really was the catalyst that got me started on TV: first on *Motorcycle Mania*, and then again a few years later when Hugh King and Original Productions decided to do the *Biker Build-Off* series for Discovery. Jesse, ever mindful of his friendships, had a hand in making sure I'd be part of that one, as well. And while the TV thing has been terrific fun and definitely good for our business, the day-in and day-out operation of the shop is still pretty much our priority, and still is what it has always been: working

Opposite page: **After more than 30 years in the industry, most builders at Dave's level no longer get their hands dirty painting and building motorcycles. Fortunately, Dave still finds the work a lot of fun.**

PPG

Here, Keith Hanson stripes some flames Dave painted. Each individual piece of sheet metal is painted and sanded dozens of times for a cue-ball finish.

hard, fabricating parts, building new bikes, and sweetening up existing bikes.

The one way the custom bike scene has changed most since I got into it back in the day is attending the big rallies, like Sturgis. I started going to Sturgis back in 1977 and I've been there every year since, but let me tell you, it wasn't the kind of family-friendly tourist spectacle it is today. It wasn't anything like what you see on the Travel Channel. I remember, real early on, hearing from Arlin Fatland (of 2-Wheelers in Denver) and Arlen Ness about how cool this little, out-of-the-way rally was way out in South Dakota. I myself had never been there. I remember Arlen called me in 1976 to tell me how great this run was in Sturgis, South Dakota, and that I should go next year. "It's like nothing else you've ever seen, or any place you've ridden a bike," Arlen told me.

Back then no one stayed in hotels because there just weren't any out in the Badlands. We all camped at Spearfish or in the Town Park, and let me tell you, the fresh air and high prairie sun must have done something to get us all fired up. It was crazy and wild at those campgrounds, and the party went on all night. I honestly wonder how any of us ever got any sleep with the stuff that went on there. You definitely didn't want to show up on a Japanese bike, because it could have gotten burned—literally, spirited off in the night and set on fire. It seems hard to believe now, but there were probably three or four Japanese bikes burned every year. Somebody would just walk up, punch a hole in the gas tank of some

Keith Hanson outlines Dave's flame paint job with gold leaf. Try doing *that* with a spray can!

Python

Flames and metalflake never go out of style when they're done right.

The Cycle Fab take on the wide tire look that has swept the custom bike world in recent years.

poor guy's Honda, toss a match, and boom! There it went. And everybody laughed about it.

I remember all kinds of naked people running around: young ones, old ones, men, and women, and guys doing burnouts on a little strip of asphalt maybe 100 feet long, right down in the center of Town Park. These motorcycle maniacs would all gather there to see who could do the sickest burnout. Everybody would be drinking, and after a while, half the guys would be completely shit-faced. They'd drop their bikes trying to rev the nuts off of them, then laugh their asses off, get up off the asphalt, and try it again. It was totally insane, so naturally, we decided to make Sturgis the site of our first official Hamster ride. We've been going back every year since.

The telling thing about Sturgis, though, is how it started to become more corporate in the late 1980s and early 1990s. It wasn't something anyone would notice at first, but by the year 2000, it had really changed. It is big business now. The city closes off the Town Park and most everybody stays at the motels and hotels that are all over the area now. There's so much corporate involvement, so much money to be made, that you don't really see the crazy, out-of-control kind of behavior you used to. It's kind of sad, in a way.

When we used to go to Sturgis, it was to let loose and hang out with our buddies, but now a lot of the time is spent doing business or working a vendor booth. Now everybody's more responsible. The vendor areas used to be a few guys selling T-shirts and bike parts (to get folks back home). Now, it's a multi-million-dollar operation with companies showing up from all over the world. They come a long way, and want to make some money, so they take the whole

Have spraygun, will travel: the shop's gas dispenser gets the full flame treatment.

thing pretty seriously. Now it's to the point that the whole week that we're at Sturgis, I only go to town once or twice at most, because there's just too much congestion, too much traffic, and too many people. It's ridiculous how popular it's become in such a short period of time. I have to say I miss the old times, but then again, I'm fully aware that times change, and people and tastes have to change as well.

I had a lot more fun going to bike events back in the early years of my career, because we builders weren't considered celebrities, we were just bikers. I used to love all that getting crazy, but I also loved the fact that you could just be yourself and ride around and talk shop. Some weekends we'd get together on our bikes and just ride someplace, like the Harley Rendezvous they had in Upstate New York every summer. That was one of the craziest places for bikers, almost as nuts as Sturgis. We'd just camp out under the stars and enjoy the madness of things happening around us, and nobody much cared what anybody else thought.

I remember once, in the early days, being so excited to make it to all the runs that, in 1979, we headed for Daytona with three bikes strapped down in the

continued on page 152

The Build-Off Build

Long, low, and very, very fast, the deep red pro-street stomper that Dave Perewitz designed, built, and rode in the second episode of the Discovery Channel's groundbreaking custom motorcycle program, *Biker Build-Off*, has quickly become Cycle Fab's signature piece. An estimated 12 million viewers caught the program as Perewitz put the skills of his shop's crew up against the Billy Lane of Florida's Choppers, Inc.

While the TV crews were only on hand for three five-day taping sessions, Dave said that finishing the actual motorcycle was a process that was a lot less camera-friendly; "All in all, it took us about three months to complete the bike and get it ready to put on the road," he said. The bike had to be built for reliability as well as style, as the show's producers had scheduled an unforgiving 1,000-mile ride from Pensacola, Florida, to an *Easyriders* custom motorcycle show in Dallas, Texas. Dave describes the ensuing cross-country trek as "one of the greatest rides I've taken in my entire life," due to the presence of several dozen of his closest friends and fellow Hamsters members.

To counter Dave's timelessly cool pro-street lowrider, Lane constructed a radical stretch chopper featuring a rigid chassis with a 20-inch seat height and a set of under-seat exhaust pipes that managed to set the young builder's jacket afire during the journey. Despite the small fire and other minor problems, Lane's bike won the people's choice vote in the competition. Since the competition, Lane and Dave have appeared at many events together.

Right: Dave finishes up a bike in the assembly room at Cycle Fab.

Opposite page: What they don't tell you on TV is that custom motorcycles done the right way are never hurried affairs.

Nevertheless, Dave's appearance on the show catapulted his popularity to unimagined heights among both custom motorcycle fans and folks who just happened to find their TV dials set on Discovery Channel that particular night. Much of that can be attributed to one very special motorbike, a machine that the builder deliberately designed to test the very limits of his skills. Among the many innovative tricks in place was a TP Engineering polished billet engine with a single carburetor breathing for each head. This required extensive machinework on the engine and a special manifold to accommodate the carbs.

The use of a Softail chassis was all part of the Cycle Fab plan to create a motorcycle that was ergonomically suited to a long, multistate ride. This particular frame was made and designed at Rolling Thunder in Canada by Dave, Big Ron, and the crew at Rolling Thunder, including Dave the engineer. Even the custom-bent, two-piece handlebars were crafted to demand very little from a seated rider; a final belt drive, as used on many stock Harley-Davidsons, was used to transfer power to the rear wheel virtually vibration-free. NASCAR engineer Gerald Rinehart built the bellowing straight-pipe exhaust system, while Dave himself designed and hammered out the voluptuous teardrop-shaped fuel cell.

"I didn't want to go with flames, because that's so classic. But I figured, what the hell, I'll do a flame paint job and add something really special to the base coat," Dave said. That something special turned out to be a hue known to racing aficionados as Mario Andretti Red, in honor of the Indy car champ who officially retired the color upon finishing his racing career in 1994. Not only did Andretti honor Perewitz by allowing Dave to use his favorite color for the show chopper, but Andretti also eventually visited Cycle Fab's newest headquarters in Bridgewater, Massachusetts, where he test-rode the motorcycle. After such an exhilarating experience, it would only seem natural for Dave to want to maintain ownership of the Build-Off machine, but he says the bike was actually sold to one of his best customers just weeks after the completion of taping.

back of our truck. We ended up hitting a blizzard along the way. When we finally made it to Florida, we pulled into the hotel parking lot and it was barely 32 degrees outside. We looked in the truck and realized that these freshly finished bikes were encased in ice that appeared to be 6 inches thick! It took a whole day before we could get enough ice melted to even get the bikes unloaded. It was completely nuts, but that's how committed we were just to being there. Sometimes I do think I've gotten used to all the comforts of life, though, and road trips and camping wouldn't be such a great idea anymore.

Though I make sure I ride all the bikes I build, I don't get much chance to put many miles on anymore, because I'm always busy with work. Most of my best riding time in recent years comes at bike events. On the rare occasion that I have got a weekend off and I'm not traveling, I'm content to head down to my place on the Cape where I can kick back and relax.

Kory Souza, often described as Dave's right-hand man, has been a creative force in the Cycle Fab dynasty.

From design to welding to complete rolling custom bikes, Cycle Fabrications has it covered.

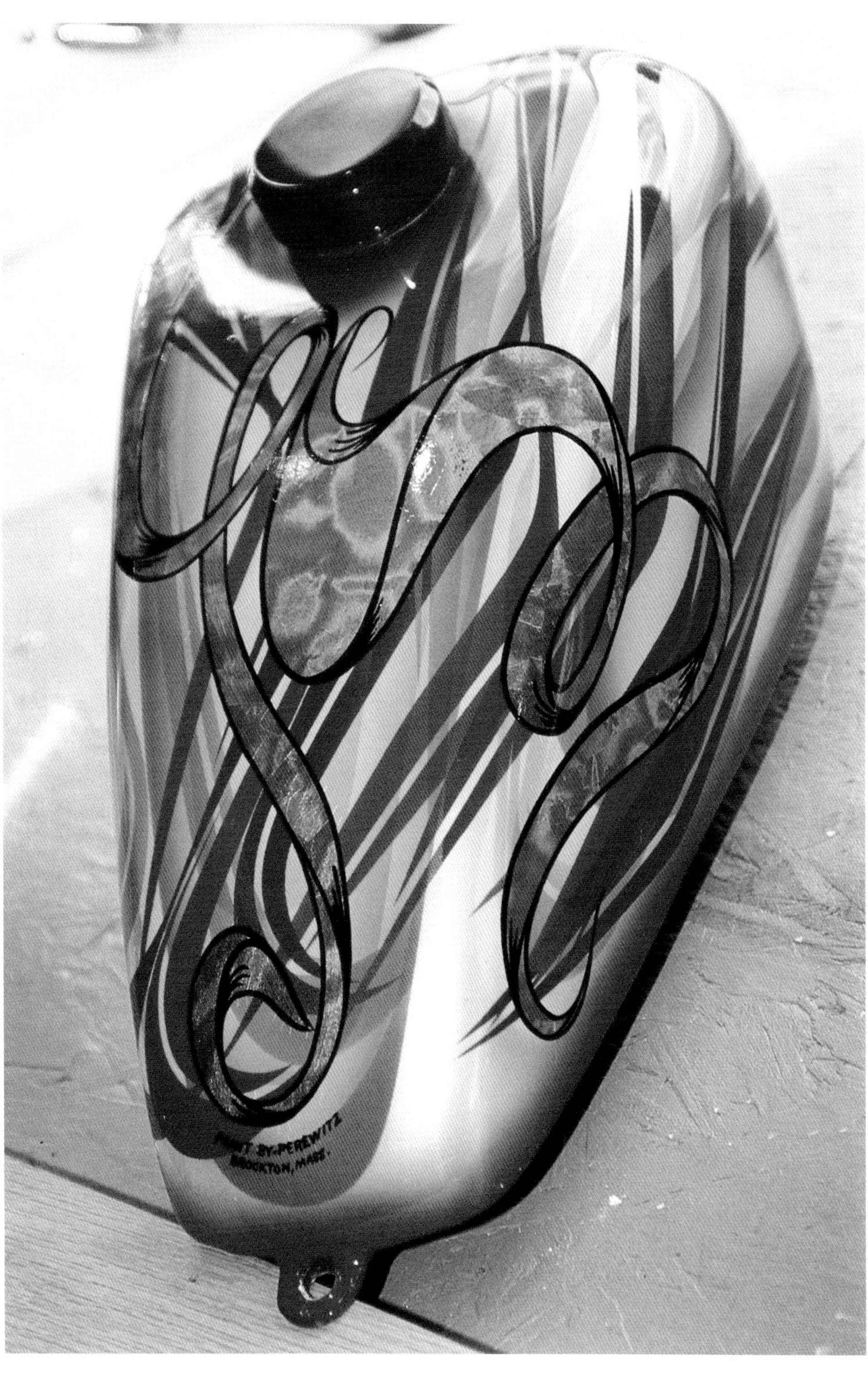

Dave first noticed the beauty and detail of gold leaf on vintage fire engines around his hometown of Brockton, Massachusetts. The design eventually made it onto his motorcycles. Dave painted this tank for his very first *Easyriders* magazine bike in 1976.

When it comes to building a bike for a customer, I still pretty much go about it in the same way I always have. I know a lot of builders like to use elaborate drawings and sketchbooks, and some guys will even do a 3-D version of a bike before they get started. For me, though, each new bike we build doesn't even get any sketches because I lay it all out in my head. When a customer comes to me, all I need is a few hours to talk and mull it over. After an hour or two of hearing his ideas of what kind of bike he'd like, I've pretty much got the design worked out in my mind. Of course, the hard part is transferring that design to the crew and getting it made.

I do consider myself very lucky to have had such a talented crew to work with over the years. We've been together so long now that even though I don't write down my ideas or sketch anything, they just sort of intuitively know what's up. Keith Hanson, who does all my artwork, is a guy I've worked beside for so long we're on the exact same wavelength when it comes to fleshing out ideas. Ron Landers, AKA Big Ron, who has been with me to many years too count, contributes his magic to the fabrication of the bikes. When it's time for paint after Big Ron's magic and I don't have time, Jay Crone gets the base coats painted for Keith and me. It's the custom bike builder's equivalent to being able to finish each other's sentences. And because of this, with the crew's input, the finished product is usually better than what I originally had in mind—they're that good.

Over the years we've worked on a lot of stock Harley-Davidson frames, some because many customers just didn't have the money to completely replace their stock chassis. In these cases, the customer will have us redo their stock chassis with a weld-on Hardtail or a new front raked neck section. Even with all the great aftermarket chassis components available, we still do that kind of work. For example, we even designed our own jigs for straightening frames because after you weld on new sections or cut and re-rake a frame, it just won't ride right if the frame isn't true. I'm sure it sounds like a lot of work, but that's the way we've always done it, and that's the way we always want to do it.

As for where we get our ideas, one thing I always tell young guys who want to get into this kind of work is that they have to be open to all kinds of influences, even the ordinary things they see in their houses on a daily basis (like appliances or toys, just the familiar shapes of everyday objects). If you're really

Opposite page: **One of Dave's creations on display in front of the new Cycle Fab facility.**

Above: **A bike waits its turn at the new service department.**

Pro-street chopper, Cycle Fab style, means a bike that looks mean but rides as comfortably as any stocker. Dave built this bike for the Leukemia Society in a joint venture with NASCAR team owner Ray Evernham and PPG.

excited about a project and if you're feeling creative, you can look just about anywhere for inspiration. It's not uncommon that I'll find myself looking hard at a billboard as I drive along the road on the way to work. Many of the gold leaf designs and scrollwork that I've used were all taken from old fire engines I saw as a kid, which just goes to show how random it can all be.

Maybe I'll even find ideas in hot rod magazines, because as much as some bike guys try to deny it, there is, and always has been, an incredible amount of artistic crossover between the two schools. If building custom motorcycles is something that's always on your mind, you'll always find something to inspire you. But even then, all the influences in the world won't help unless you're committed to living this way. The secret that all new, young builders need to learn is that they have to be willing to play this game, not just as a job, but as a lifestyle. You can't just act like a builder, you have to think like a builder, and you have to feel like a builder.

People ask me sometimes how I came to be so closely associated with the whole long-stretched, "the Look" bikes. The best explanation I can give is that it came about as the result of styles changing over the years. Guys like me are always looking for new, innovative styles, and when we got to pro-street style, we all decided we'd found a style that really looked cool. It had that certain style that all the choppers and bobbers had, but they were also fast and handled pretty

well because of the low-slung chassis and short front ends. Plus, they were comfortable to ride. These were the custom motorcycles you could just get on and go where you wanted.

And the bikes are better. The ride on a modern, pro-street custom is very different from what a stroker used to be. The engines are so much smoother and more powerful. At best, even with a big-inch motor 30 years ago, you had an engine that made maybe 70 horsepower. That's nothing compared to the 100-plus ponies these bikes are putting out today. The frames are a lot stronger these days, too, with most of the main manufacturers using heavy-walled mild steel. As a result, the bikes ride a lot better, they're way smoother, and they don't vibrate nearly as much.

I hear a lot about some younger guys who don't like the high-end customs, but I'm still content to build the bobbers, choppers, whatever anybody wants. I know about the new rat-bike movement that a lot of young guys are into, and

Dave and Jody blowing off some steam on an afternoon ride. The crew has less time to cruise as the shop has become more popular.

Looking more like one of the early custom bobbers that ruled the roads back when Dave was just starting his career, this green rigid ride is timelessly cool. Check out the dished gas tanks and the sprung saddle. Where's Marlon Brando to claim his bike?

that's fine for them, but I just can't bring myself to build raggedy-looking shit. But some people are really into that, and the bikes they're turning out are at least fairly well-built and definitely unusual. There's still room for a lot of innovation and ideas, and if you really like custom motorcycles, you'll find something to like in all kinds of styles.

While I'm known for pro-street, choppers, and baggers (or as we call them "baggas"), back when stretch choppers were all the rage, I put on the longest forks I've ever used on a bike: it was a 19-inch-over springer back in 1971. As you'd imagine, the bike handled about as well as a seesaw with wheels, but I didn't mind because we were young and didn't know any better! Later on, I'd extended the neck of that bike 12 inches and put 40 degrees of rake in the neck, still using that 19-inch-over stock springer.

(Raked triple trees are something I have never been a proponent of. They will help change the way your bike sits and rides with a long front end, but too many people are under the impression that they can bolt on a set of raked trees rather than raking the frame. Raking the frame is a lot more time consuming and harder to get perfect, but there's no substitute for proper geometry to make a long chopper work effectively.)

Although a lot of guys will no longer work on stock bikes once they start building ground-up custom motorcycles, I'll still do a Road Glide or a bagger every now and then when somebody asks me. I like to take on projects like that because it shows people that you can start with a stock bike, do anything you want to it, and still make it ride well on the road. One of the bikes we built for Brad Whitford of Aerosmith that ended up in an issue of *Easyriders* magazine started out as a stock 2003 Harley-Davidson Fat Boy. From a strictly technical standpoint, there isn't much left of the stock bike. We ended up chopping up the frame, using only the seat area, downtubes, and the cradle of the motor; everything else we built from scratch. That bike got a Phatail kit for a wider rear tire and was lowered to ride more comfortably, and Brad loves it.

But while I'll occasionally customize a stock Harley, I don't pay too much attention to the bikes that come straight out of the factory. I will admit I've always admired the Ducatis, because the Italian bikes are so well designed and detailed so

Dave catching some wind with Natalie Jackson, motocross champion and host of ESPN's *Chopper Nation.*

nicely. My neighbor and friend Tom Savini, who's an ex racer, rants and raves about his Ducati. When he was buying it he said to me he was either "going big or going home." I have ridden with him a few times and can see from behind him or in front of him that Ducatis are a well-handling and -made machine.

The new motorcycles I see from Harley-Davidson are pretty much just copies of what I and other custom motorcycle builders have been doing for years, so what's there to learn? I mean, they've always copied from us (and never once given us any credit), so what point is there in trying to get any ideas from the manufacturers? You never know what you'll see from the factory in a few years—though you might get an idea if you watch what the custom builders are doing—but I can assure you that you wouldn't see the kinds of stock bikes you see today if the big corporations hadn't studied us for so long.

Some of the other builders get additional kicks from doing paintings on canvas or sculptures, but I never have really done much art outside of the bike

continued on page 167

All work and some play: Dave spends an evening going over the books in his Cycle Fab office.

Gibson Guitars Chopper

While many luminaries of the new generation of chopper builders take competition between individual builders as seriously as NASCAR drivers do with the guy in the rearview mirror, Dave Perewitz and his old-school contemporaries still enjoy working together. When Dave was asked to join longtime friends and fellow custom bike legends Donnie Smith and Arlen Ness to craft a motorcycle and an electric guitar for a promotion sponsored by the Gibson Guitar Company, it was cause for celebration. "Here are two of the guys in the industry I admire and respect the most, and we get to have fun doing a bike *and* a guitar. I mean how much better does it get than that?" Dave asked.

In fact, for custom choppers built and displayed during the 2003 season, few bikes could touch the trio of flamed and raked-out machines delivered to Gibson's corporate headquarters. Dave's machine took points for its cool purple undercoat, detailed with a series of slick orange and yellow flames; power throbbed courtesy of a TP Engineering 124-ci motor, with a 280-mm, or 10.5-inch-wide, rear Performance Machine wheel soaking up the torque.

Roland Sands, who would later become a formidable chopper builder in his own right, helped design the unique billet wheels that featured tines shaped like the necks and heads of Gibson guitars. It was all part of an incredible year for Dave, who had earlier been named Best Custom Motorcycle Builder/Fabricator by the staff and readers of *Easyriders* magazine. The promotion, titled Three Kings of Custom, was organized by motojournalist Beau Allen Pacheco, who had played a Gibson axe during his early years as a singer/comedian in Las Vegas. With the Three Kings signature series guitars already commanding top dollar from collectors, it's obvious the promotion was a success—and a move that revealed the depth of the appeal of custom motorcycles.

Left: **Now Perewitz's fans can make music on or off their motorcycles.**

Opposite page: **Flames, choppers, and rock and roll guitars: three ingredients that will never go out of style!**

The advent of computer-controlled milling machines allowed the creation of cool parts like these guitar-spoked wheels from performance machines.

Miniature guitar-shaped rearview mirrors add to the craftsmanship of the Perewitz guitar chop.

Rare company: Dave Perewitz with the Gibson Guitars chopper. He was one of three custom motorcycle builders selected to take part in the historic collaboration.

shop. I do like to work with my spray guns, though, and from time to time will try something different, like the 2-foot-tall wine bottle I did for a friend who owns an Italian restaurant. We painted it with flames just like the ones you'd see on one of my bikes. He's had that bottle sitting on his bar for years, and people who know about motorcycles can see that it's one of my designs. We also flamed out my daughter Jody's surf board. She has the coolest board on the beach.

Over the years I've painted flames on everything from trash cans to water skis to the front of my building, and even a lamppost. I flamed the mailbox at my house. I've always been amazed that people still have mailboxes vulnerable enough that kids can come along with a baseball bat and knock them down. So, out in front of my place I have a mailbox that's basically the same configuration as a standard mailbox, except it's made from quarter-inch steel plate on a base of 4-inch-square square steel tubing. Anybody whacks this with a bat, well, they're going to hurt themselves pretty good! At my Cape Cod house, I've built a full steel roll cage around the mailbox, which is pretty wild. (I may be a little obsessed with my mailboxes.) I guess I wouldn't mind spending time at art gal-

The Gibson bike bears the same purple paint job with orange flames as the limited-edition 1957 Les Paul Goldtop guitar—the bike, however, sounds better!

leries and stuff like that, but I don't have all that much time and manage to have a lot of fun just working on projects like these.

For as much press and attention as it's received up until now, it's hard to fathom that the first of Discovery's *Biker Build-Off* shows were kept very quiet. It wasn't like it was the talk of the industry or anything like it is now; at the time, people just heard that Billy Lane was doing a show for Discovery Channel with Roger Bourget, and maybe they should check it out. There wasn't much hubbub when the show first aired, either. The hype actually started building up afterward, when the people who saw it for the first time realized how cool it was to see these guys they'd only read about in magazines building their choppers on TV.

Interest in custom motorcycles really started going crazy after I did episode two of *Biker Build-Off*. It seemed like all of a sudden everybody started watching the show, even people who had never even ridden a motorcycle or had ever wanted anything to do with bikes. I was, and still am, surprised at how well the whole thing has been accepted by everyday people. Before the whole TV phenomenon broke big, you wouldn't have thought the average Joe Homemaker or housewife would ever watch a show like that, but the fact that ordinary folks were taking an interest in what we were doing sure took biking to a whole new direction.

Beauty by the lake: it's not hard for photographers to find fitting backdrops for such lovely subjects.

Burn-out time at Bike Night at Cycle Fab in Bridgewater, Massachusetts, held on the third Wednesday of each month. Don't worry, the shop can sell this customer a spare!

Because of the popularity of the show and some other TV projects we've been involved in over the years, we now have people stopping by the shop all the time—and not just from around here in New England, but from all over the country. I take as much time as I can to speak with them, and sometime the staff will come get me if I'm busy and I'll sign T-shirts for them or take a picture. I get asked for an autograph sometimes when I'm out with my family, and I always try to take the time to do it for them. It's great that so many people truly appreciate what we do.

A lot of guys are really bothered by having a TV production crew in their shops while they're trying to work, but it never really bothers me. Discovery comes in, sets up its cameras, and we just go to work like it's an otherwise normal day. I think one of the reasons it's worked out so well for me is that I just continue doing my thing. Nobody here is trying to get on some kind of wild movie-star trip; we're still just building bikes. Though I do have to admit that it was strange to actually see our shop on TV, where I could see from someone else's point of view how I talk and interact with the other guys. It made me feel proud of how well we all work together. There was never a stressful moment because I don't get stressed at all; we're all mellow, and we all get along. The conflict and controversy may make for good TV, but our ability to work together makes for good custom bike building, and that's what I think makes Cycle Fab so special.

Jody Perewitz built and designed this cool burgundy bobber that serves as her everyday ride.

"One of the things in my career I'm proudest of: my induction into the American Motorcyclist Association's Hall of Fame."

One of the reasons I think choppers have captured the imagination of the American public is the intrigue and the mystique of being a Harley rider. There's still this whole image that surrounds it, and when some people see it on TV, they become irresistibly attracted to the world of custom bikes, and everything that goes with it. These people are bringing biker culture into the mainstream. And though this has been growing for the better part of 10 years, the biker mystique has recently attracted thousands more new weekend bikers to riding. I find myself building quite a few bikes for well-heeled guys who are new to the sport. Now there are all sorts of lawyers, executives, and doctors riding and buying custom bikes.

I've built bikes for a lot of NASCAR guys, too, over the years. These are guys who really understand creativity in engineering. They're some of my favorite customers, because when they smile and show how much they like what you've done for them, you really know you've done your job. The cool thing about them is how enthusiastic

they are about it. When people find their way to biking kind of late in life, so to speak, very often they're overwhelmed and then consumed with how cool the so-called freedom of the road really is.

If I had to list my proudest professional accomplishment it would be being inducted into not one, but *three* different motorcycling halls of fame. I was named to the Hall of Fame at Sturgis, the National Motorcyclists' Hall of Fame, and I got a medal from the American Motorcyclist Association in Ohio when I was inducted into its Hall of Fame a few years ago. Getting into the Hall of Fame didn't mean much to me until I got in, but once I was in, it became pretty important. I'm lucky that my mom is still alive to see all of this. She's pretty proud of us, and my father, who passed away a few years back, was proud too. He kept a big collection of magazines and clippings about me all those years, and he'd bring them out and show people from time to time.

In another five years' time, I don't really see myself doing more bikes than I do today. At 12 or maybe 15 a year, that's the right number to keep everything

under control. I will admit that I could see endorsing some products and maybe hosting my own TV show, because we're always coming up with something new at the shop, and the work we do really lends itself to the television format.

As for the custom motorcycle game, well, hopefully in the next few years we'll see it weed out all the guys who don't belong here, people building substandard bikes and putting poorly made products out there on the market; people can get hurt if you don't do it right. Guys like that give all of us a bad name, no matter how successful we are or how good a reputation we have. A lot of good people want in because of the TV exposure, too, like a young guy who called recently from Canada. I can remember when I was just like him, young and hungry with lots of ideas and an ability to see it through to a solid, finished product. As long as these builders are willing to do it the right way, and not just for money and the glory, I think they could really add something to the game.

Opposite page: **Signing an autographed poster for a youthful fan at an industry show. Exposure on TV shows like Discovery's *Biker Build-Off* has introduced Dave's work to a new generation of bike nuts.**

Above: **A lineup of living custom bike legends: (right to left) Roger Bourget, Kendall Johnson, Donnie Smith, Cory Ness, and Dave Perewitz.**

Kory Souza's radical stretch chopper shows its narrow, wasp-waisted gas tank. Choppers displaying this kind of radical frame geometry were impossible to conceive just 25 years ago, but modern technology has made them a reality.

Chapter Five

Above: Dave on the bike with which he won Discovery Channel's *Biker Build-Off* at the Sturgis motorcycle rally in August, 2006.

Right: "People don't think we build bobbers. Well, this is a Perewitz bobber."

The Beginning of a New Beginning

PPG
CUSTOM
REFINISH TEAM

With the launch of the Discovery Channel *Biker Build-Off* in 2003, I realized I was missing the boat. We were selling T-shirts and apparel like crazy at shows, but not at home. The small retail store I had was just mainly for doing bike deals. We didn't even have regular hours. I was up there faithfully just about every Wednesday, Thursday, and Friday when I was home, but it was never the same time. In other words, it was hard for someone local to buy a shirt or ask questions or buy parts. That's when I decided I really needed to get a big retail location.

I had been looking for new space for quite some time, but not constantly. I found a few places here and there, but they were never perfect. I had heard through the town grapevine that Butch O'Brien was considering selling his property. This property was perfect—well, it *would* be perfect. It was about a mile from my house and on a busy street in a nice area. The building, though, was another story. It was an 18-wheeler garage. In other words, it was a mess. I think Susan almost fell over when I showed her the property I wanted to buy.

The building had trucks and junk everywhere, the parking lot was mostly dirt with tar scattered here and there, the paint was all peeling, and there were animals everywhere. I knew that I could make it awesome!

Well, I did just that. Once all the junk was removed, it was time to start working on the building. We tore down walls in the current bays, installed a

Opposite page: **Dave and Mario Andretti at the party for *Biker Build-Off II.***

Dave and Billy riding through Louisiana while filming *Biker Build-Off.*

state-of the art spraybooth, made a fabrication side, and started the addition. We added a 1,200-square-foot showroom with offices and a kitchen. I oversaw all the construction, and when I wasn't there Jim Leahy took over. Jim was my right-hand man when all the construction was going on.

We wanted to be open before Christmas 2004. We had set a date for a big Christmas party and open house. There were flyers all over town advertising the event and postcards were sent out. That date came too fast. The day and night and morning before the Christmas party we worked our butts off. I had people everywhere helping out. The floor guys finished that night and we painted all the walls, hung a few things up, and set up the showroom. Jesse, Jody, and Kory Souza worked till about 4 in the morning finishing everything. We went home, got about two hours of sleep, and came back to add the finishing touches.

Dave with Mario Andretti, Dave's son Jesse, and his mother, Marie Perewitz.

It was an awesome day. The building looked great, the weather was sunny but cold, we had everything out on display, and over 1,000 people came to see the new shop and buy T-shirts and gifts. I had several people tell me that they couldn't believe what I had turned this building into. I still hear it today. I guess it is kind of like a motorcycle: you have to be able to envision what it is going to turn out like.

Today, the business is doing well. I think this was the best move I have made. Every aspect of the business is done here on the same property. We have a fabrication, paint, assembly, service, and parts department. We get lots of local business as well as travelers who mark it on the trips as a destination.

Every third Wednesday of the summer months, we have bike night. People come from all over the place to "hang out" at the Perewitz's place. Last month in June we had over 1,000 bikes here. It was crazy! Bikes were parked on the lawn, in the woodchips, everywhere! We had Steve Leahy from Bear Air

Dave riding his second Discovery bike. This one won the *Biker Build-Off.*

doing airbrushed tattoos on everyone from big to small, there was burnouts, and great food cooked by Dante Mastropietro, Jesse, and his friend Bob Mello. We also had Kryptonite here giving away bike locks. Our bike nights just keep getting better!

All my kids work here at the business. My son Jesse runs the parts department, my daughter, Jody, handles all the marketing and ordering, while Jaren works in the showroom. Kory Souza, who has worked here for about four years, handles all the service work while picking up any slack where it is needed. He is definitely my right-hand man. When there is a last-minute thing to do, Kory is always available to do it. My wife does the book-keeping and handles all of the money. I guess she knows all too well I would just spend it. She also makes us some great lunches and dinners when we are working late to get bikes finished or schoolwork done.

The fender of Dave's first Discovery bike before he painted it.

Dave after competing against Indian Larry, Billy Lane, and Kendall Johnson in NASCAR race cars. Dave was leading, but he thought a black flag meant for Billy was for him so he slowed down and Kendall passed him for the win. This photo was taken the day before Indian Larry died.

My daughter, Jody, just graduated from Bridgewater State College. She juggled school and full-time work, for several years. Jody graduated with a political science degree—which I told her was going to be useful to the business someday—I just don't know when. She had plans to go to law school, but I think the motorcycle industry reeled her in. She is part of the whole industry, not just here.

Kory, Jody, and Jesse also travel to the shows around the country on weekends, meeting everyone in the industry. We travel so much that the motorcycle industry is like one big family. We look forward to seeing friends in different states and at different events when we travel. We don't get full ground-up custom jobs at events. It's more of a T-shirt seller, but it is good exposure. The more someone sees your name, the better they recognize it.

We have already started filming for our second Discovery Channel *Biker Build-Off.* I want to spend the whole day showing the cameras the new shop and all the wicked cool stuff I have collected or flamed out over the years. The build is coming along great! We have had the cameras rolling for a total of six days, with four to go. When we're finished, the bike will go to Des Moines, Iowa, and I'll ride it from there to Sturgis, South Dakota. The ride should be great. I will have Jesse, Jody, and Kory riding with me along the way. Remember, "Vote for Dave"!

Side Note

By Susan Perewitz

After much encouragement from Dave and Jody, I decided to write a side note. I gave a lot of thought to what my contribution would be to this book, and I came up with the following.

We, the Perewitz family, are and always have been a true biker family. Our kids, Jesse, Jody, and Jaren, and our almost, son-in-law, Kory, have joined us and have helped turn our business around.

The weakest part of our motorcycle business was in service and parts, because most everyone knew the name Perewitz and made the connection to custom motorcycles. Our service and parts department has grown a great deal since we turned the reins over to Jesse, the parts manager, and Kory, the service manager.

This business has allowed us to meet some wicked, awesome people and has taken us to new & exciting places in the USA and out of the country as well. *All* of our "vacations" have centered around motorcycle events. We have traveled to most all of the 48 contiguous United States and abroad to Germany, England, Hawaii, and Puerto Rico. Despite being busy with the event that took us away from home, we managed to find a small amount of time to scuba-dive in Hawaii, snorkel in Puerto Rico, visit old cathedrals in Germany, and visit Buckingham Palace. While in England, we spent half a day touring the Avon Tyre factory in Bath. Oh, what fun that was for the girls! But that's OK, 'cause we got to do lots of shopping at Harrod's of London. WooHoo!!

NASCAR's Gary Nelson's bike sits under a pile of snow because someone forgot to push it in the shop before the snow fell.

Opposite: Jody posing with her Panhead in front of the mural Bill Streeter painted on the service-department door

We are, as I said previously, a tried-and-true biker family: motorcycles are the only business we know and do. We do not have another business to fall back on during slow times. We do not own or operate a restaurant, bar, trucking company, auto repair, auto body, construction, electrical, plumbing, vehicle dealerships, banks, coffee shops, or convenience stores. This motorcycle business is the mainstay of our occupation and that is how we earn our living. The climate in New England does not make this an easy business. The short riding season of this area can be a good thing and a bad thing. Bad because we do not have year-round

riding, and good because it gives us a longer time frame to design and develop custom motorcycles.

Dave has been in the motorcycle industry for 30-plus years and shows no sign of slowing down. I appreciate "Uncle" Bob Clark's truthful and supportive ways, but he made one mistake . . . I stayed in the hospital an extra three days with Jesse, waiting for Dave to pick us up on his way home from Laconia. And by the way, Uncle Bob must have forgotten the 25 lobsters the guys bought for me to cook the first night home with my new baby boy. Men . . . Guys . . . gotta love 'em.

Above Dave used this Daytec FXR touring bike as his daily ride for a while.

Left: Dave with Aerosmith's Brad Whitford

Dave with NASCAR driver Jeremy Mayfield and exhaust guru Gerald Rinehart.

Dave with his family in the shop.

Index